PATHS TO THE PRESENT

This book is dedicated to Douglass Adair and Martin Diamond, who, by precept and example, have encouraged students at the Claremont Graduate School to probe the contemporary meaning of America's past.

Paths to the Present:

THOUGHTS ON THE CONTEMPORARY RELEVANCE OF AMERICA'S PAST

THOMAS J. OSBORNE
FRED R. MABBUTT

JOHN WILEY & SONS

New York · London · Sydney · Toronto

Library of Congress Cataloging in Publication Data:

Osborne, Thomas J.   1942–
  Paths to the Present.

  Includes bibliographical references.
   1.   United States--History—1945–   I. Mabbutt,
Fred R., 1936–   joint author.   II. Title.

E741.084 1974   917.3'03'92   73-19963
ISBN 0-471-65721-2
ISBN 0-471-65709-3 (pbk.)

Printed in the United States of America

10 9 8 7 6 5 4 3 2 1

"History is a dialogue in the present
with the past about the future."

DOUGLASS GREYBILL ADAIR
(1912–1968)

FOREWORD

This is a different—and a successful—history text. It has obviously been based on a most important assumption: the problems each of us has to confront every day, in both our personal and public lives, can best be analyzed and solved when we understand that they have their roots in the past. Whether we like it or not, whether we choose to understand it or not, history shapes our present. This is a truism. As the cliché runs, history is relevant.

Yet many have failed to see the truism or the relevance. Throughout the late 1960s enrollments in history courses dropped nationwide. The decline of interest was not due solely to the quality of classroom teaching because it was by no means limited to the college generation. Older scholars also wondered aloud whether the technology, counterculture, and new politics of the 1960s marked a major break with the American past. Some even argued that the new world was so different that the tradition of the older instructing the younger would have to be reversed, for it was the young who best understood this brave new world because they had no historical preconceptions to distort their perception of what was really going on. The ways in which we had previously seen and categorized our experience, this argument went, were simply not helpful in understanding the technological society and the manner in which it had transformed everything from politics to music to personal ethics. The "greening of America," to use the title of one of the more popular books, would occur as each of us became personally aware of what the new society offered us. For this we needed little historical perspective. Indeed, history only got in the way of the greening process, for historical experience tended to teach us the limits, the restraints, and the failures endured by earlier generations. Because their experience had taken place in a pretechnocratic, precountercultural era, it had little relevance to the new era that was to begin in the 1960s. Or so too many people believed.

History refused to be buried, however. As this book goes to press, the daily newspaper has to give a history lesson in addition to its recital of current events. The Watergate fiasco can be debated only in terms of the kinds of personal rights or the magnitude of presidential power the Founding Fathers of 200 years ago intended us to have. United States foreign policies, as directed by presidential advisor Henry Kissinger, cannot be comprehended without some understanding of nineteenth-century balance-of-power politics. Popular music is increasingly influenced by nostalgia for the 1940s and 1950s, traditional country music, and even the chants and rhythms associated with centuries-old Eastern mysticism. It has been discovered that the greening of a society, like the greening of a plant, requires roots. Americans are once again examining their roots.

This book contributes significantly to that examination. With sound scholarship and a clear style, Professors Osborne and Mabbutt have helped us to a better understanding of nine of the central problems in contemporary America. They do this by tracing historical development (as in feminist movements and environmental concerns) or by comparing the present problem with earlier, comparable examples (such as Populism and revolution). They have discovered that some of our national characteristics have had amazing endurance and ability to shape our present. The Puritan ethic provides a striking example. They also show, as in the case of the American Revolution or the new isolationism in foreign policy, that what we often consider to be a valid historical analogy is actually a misleading, distorted, hence dangerous, way of thinking about some of our problems.

The authors, then, have made a dual contribution. They have given us a book in which history is not a dry recital of facts but an illumination that is absolutely necessary if we are to see and understand clearly what is happening right now. They have done this with impressive scholarship and a grasp of the historical process itself. Because history refuses to be buried, and none of us can escape his past, it is best that we try to understand it. This book shows how to go about performing this most important task.

WALTER LaFEBER
Cornell University

PREFACE

History professors are asked continually by their students in survey courses: "why study history"? And just as often historians have responded that "we study the past in order to gain perspective on the present." Although the reply is not incorrect, the frequency with which the question is raised indicates that the stock answer is not satisfactory, possibly because the proposition is seldom applied to demonstrate how the past is connected with the present.

A major reason for this unfortunate circumstance is that most history textbooks do not discuss the contemporary relevance of the past. An example from Lewis Carroll's fantasy, *Alice in Wonderland*, provides a sad commentary on how history was and is approached by most scholars. The tiny creatures of Wonderland are swimming in a pool of tears shed by a lost and confused Alice. As the dormouse emerged from this pool he assures his friends, "I'll get you dry. I'll tell you the dryest thing I know." Then he proceeds to recite: "In 1066 William the Conquerer. . . ."

In recent years, however, remarkable improvements have been made in the quality of college history texts. Students are responding to the new interpretive and analytical accounts that are "issue-oriented" and not simply compilations of facts. But even these "issue books" tend to ignore the contemporary relevance of history. Americans in general and college students in particular are looking for a usable past—one that will help them gain a better understanding of the present. It is our underlying assumption that the study of the past will not only furnish perspective for viewing the present but will simultaneously help us to formulate a course of action for the future.

The Founding Fathers recognized this truth, as the late Douglass Adair pointed out, and in 1787 utilized history as a tool for constructing a more perfect union.° Martin Diamond, Adair's former colleague at the Claremont Graduate School, carried this point further by claiming that a deep understanding of *The Federalist* papers is indispensable for the resolution of our constitutional difficulties today.† If more scholars do not follow the example of Adair and Diamond, we can be assured that history will be regarded even more as an anachronism and the question "why study history?" will go begging.

This book is designed primarily for those students who wish to determine how and why American history is relevant to the contemporary scene. It is no substitute for the narrative, documentary, or "issue-oriented" texts. Instead, it is a brief supplemental work intended for the use of students taking introductory courses in American history and government, many of whom will forget the facts and interpretations they have studied unless some "paths to the present" are discerned.

Our book is divided into nine chapters, each of which relates a major historical issue to American life since World War II. Historians, for good reason, have customarily treated the period after 1945 as a new era. Although there are no absolute discontinuities in history, the postwar generation does exhibit some unique contours.

In many ways it has been preoccupied with its own assumptions, problems, and aspirations. The advent of the Nuclear Age has forced Americans to re-examine their old views of conventional warfare. The isolationist impulse that has been so influential in shaping America's diplomatic tradition has been nearly abandoned in lieu of global involvement—the Nixon Doctrine notwithstanding. In the sphere of domestic politics we have witnessed the vast proliferation of federally sponsored welfare programs during the last two and one-half decades. Racial tensions and urban problems have been particularly acute, and discontent among the young has reached

---

*Douglass G. Adair, " ' Experience Must be Our Only Guide': History, Democratic Theory, and the United States Constitution," in Ray Allen Billington, Ed., *The Reinterpretation of Early American History* (New York: Norton, 1968), pp. 129–150.

†Martin Diamond, "Democracy and The Federalist: A Reconsideration of the Framers' Intents," *The American Political Science Review*, **LIII**, I (March 1959), 52–68.

unprecedented proportions. Automation and cybernation have assumed increasing importance. The shift from a production to a service economy has been another arresting feature of the postwar years. John Kenneth Galbraith asserts that a "New Class" of Americans, well-educated and nonmaterially inclined, has emerged. In short, the year 1945 marks a watershed and the period that follows constitutes a time package which we have treated as America's contemporary scene.

The chronological demarcation dictates only part of the organizational format. To achieve a balance in subject matter we have selected key topics from a relatively broad range of areas. Chapter 1 deals with our social and cultural heritage by showing how the Puritan Ethic continues to shape American values in the 1970s. Chapter 2 treats the ways in which today's young radicals are using the Revolution of 1776 to bring about fundamental changes in our political system. This segment is followed by a consideration of the philosophical problems involved in framing a constitution. Rexford Tugwell's document is compared and contrasted with the Madisonian model of the eighteenth century. In Chapter 4 the old isolationism of the agrarian republic is considered as a prospective foreign policy for the American superstate of the late twentieth century. Chapter 5 looks at the doctrine of political equality contained in the Declaration of Independence and the Constitution and measures that promise against two centuries of white racism. Present discrimination against women and the tendency to overlook their role in shaping American history are key themes in Chapter 6. In Chapter 7 the old Populism of the 1890s is compared and contrasted with its counterpart of the 1970s. Chapter 8 examines the historical antecedents of today's ecology crusade, and Chapter 9 speculates about the threat that modern technology may pose to our civil liberties in the twenty-first century.

Works that utilize a comparative approach assume the risk of sacrificing continuity for relevance. Take this particular book, for example: the reader who is unable to discern important connections between Puritanism, the American Revolution, and the Constitution, must have a disjointed and truncated view of the past. Relevance is important, but so is a sense of historical continuity. To achieve both we have inserted transitional paragraphs between the chapters.

In this way the greatest virtue of traditional textbooks (a sense of continuity) is retained and their major defect (a lack of relevance) is avoided. We think our readers will find that the challenge of relevancy has been met in a sensible and provocative manner.

THOMAS J. OSBORNE

FRED R. MABBUTT

Claremont, California

ACKNOWLEDGMENTS

Throughout the two years it took to conceive and write this book a host of friends and colleagues have generously given their assistance. In the difficult planning stage we were given needed encouragement and suggestions by Thom Hendrickson and his colleagues on the History faculty at Cerritos College. After the project moved from the blueprint to the production phase our editors, Carl Beers and Wayne Anderson, deftly handled the matter of securing and evaluating chapter reviews. In most instances these reviews were very helpful; in some they were excellent. Special recognition in this area goes to Walter LaFeber, Mary C. Lynn, and Theodore G. Neima.

With respect to making the final manuscript more polished and readable, we wish to acknowledge the stalwart efforts of our colleagues at Santa Ana College, Lee N. Layport and Richard Sneed. Because of his insistance on clarity and logic in exposition, we owe a special debt of gratitude to Michael V. Fox, who, in spite of his heavy administrative schedule at Chapman College, always found time to read another page or an additional chapter. Dorothy M. Osborne deserves tribute for typing and proofreading much of the manuscript. Ultimately we are most indebted to our wives, Sheila and Carol, who for two years suffered neglect while they critiqued our material and offered indispensable encouragement. For whatever errors of fact and judgment that may be found we alone are responsible.

We should also like to express our gratitude to various academic journals in which material appearing in this book has been published. Special thanks are accorded to Professor Paul Carter, editor of the *Colorado Quarterly*, who published several sections of the manuscript in his periodical and from whose editorial suggestions we have greatly benefited. Other parts of our work have appeared in *Thought: A Journal of Culture and Idea* (Fordham University), *The Centennial Review* (Michigan State University), *The New Orleans Review* (Loyola University, New Orleans, Louisiana), *The Texas Quarterly* (University of Texas, Austin), *Forum* (Ball State University), and *Current.*

CONTENTS

Human life is reduced to real suffering, to hell, only when two ages, two cultures and religions overlap. . . . There are times when a whole generation is caught in this way between two modes of life, with the consequence that it loses all power to understand itself and has no standard, no security, no simple acquiescence.

Hermann Hesse
Steppenwolf

ONE

THE PURITAN ETHIC
IN POSTWAR AMERICA

THOMAS J. OSBORNE

It was the plight of Harry Haller, the brooding protagonist in Hermann Hesse's novel *Steppenwolf,* to live through an age of chaotic change. Surely Haller's predicament is not unfamiliar to Americans living in the postwar era. America's rapid transition from a nineteenth-century rural agrarian state to an urbanized technetronic leviathan has astonished, mesmerized, and numbed recent generations. Our environment alters more each decade than it has in centuries. The accelerating velocity of this change, especially during the last 25 years, has produced a widespread cultural malady that one writer has aptly termed "future shock." [1] At one time or another most thoughtful people can lament with Harry Haller that there seems to be "no standard, no security, no simple acquiescence."

This was not always the case. There was a time in our nation's not too distant past when change seemed gradual and society's norms and institutions meshed rather smoothly with the slowly advancing state of technology. If it can be said that America's traditional norms and institutions were the product of any dominant ethical system it would be that adopted by our seventeenth-century Puritan fore-fathers. The Puritan ethic was clearly defined and somewhat rigid in matters concerning work, leisure, sexual conduct, child rearing, and the treatment of elders. Although these standards of human conduct led in some instances to blatant repression and hypocrisy, there was little confusion about what constituted deviant behavior. [2] There was a pervading certainty and orderliness about life that seemed natural and assuring. As Calvinist theology went bankrupt during the eighteenth and nineteenth centuries the Puritan ethic was secularized into what became known as the "gospel of success" and "Victorian morality." Nevertheless, the basic Puritan values of a receding agrarian age remained intact and were carried into the twentieth century with the rising tide of moralistic, middle-class Progressivism.

Disillusionment among the "Lost Generation" intellectuals of the 1920s led to a bitter assault on Puritan morality, but the diatribes of Malcolm Cowley and H. L. Mencken were not so damaging to the old moral verities as the emerging mass culture. America's early modern culture, the Jazz Age, was diffused throughout the country by commercial radio, photographs, motion pictures, telephones, and automobiles. By the 1920s American technology had spawned a consumption-oriented society with an insatiable appetite for labor-saving appliances and commercial entertainment. This was a water-shed decade that repudiated the values of rural, farm-oriented, Protestant America. [3] The exigencies of depression and war provid-ed impetus for a shift in the national mood. Concern for the country's precarious morale gradually began to eclipse the debate over moral-ity. During the postwar years new technological advances in elec-trification and biological chemistry raised agonizing questions about the relevance of America's old values. The traditional Puritan ethic, which President Nixon recently trumpeted before a conference of Republican governors at colonial Williamsburg, has encountered automation and the new morality, and Americans are faced with a crucial moral dilemma.

Having defined the problem, we can now attempt to probe the origins and nature of America's ethical predicament. The impact of technological unemployment on a nation imbued with the work ethic is explored first. Then an assessment is made of the prevailing ethical confusion, especially in the matter of sexual conduct, that has resulted from biological technology and the overlapping of conflicting moral codes.

Central to the Puritan attitude toward work was the concept of a vocational "calling." According to Calvinist doctrine, God issued a dual command to human beings. The first was a general calling for man to repent and live as though he had been predestined to salvation. There was also a particular calling that required men to labor diligently at whatever occupation God had designated for them. In this manner each individual would provide for his own maintenance and serve the community as well. It is important to note that both callings were to be followed simultaneously. Without saving grace, the work of the most industrious person amounted to "nothing else in God's sight, but a beautiful abomination."[4] In the event of a conflict between the two callings the occupational was always to give way to the spiritual.

Members of the elect were not to choose a vocational calling at random; instead they were to seek out God's will in this matter. Prayer and reason would disclose to the solicitous believer those endeavors for which his skills were best suited. Because God instituted callings so that everyone might serve his community and his Maker, it followed that a Christian could perform any kind of work that was honest and socially beneficial. God enlisted the services of the swineherd as well as those of the magistrate. Socioeconomic status did not relieve anyone from the responsibility of pursuing a vocational calling. Wealthy and talented men could not enjoy the benefits of a commonwealth without contributing to its welfare. John Cotton probably had the Bay Colony oligarchs in mind when he exhorted:

> If thou beest a man that lives without a calling, though thou
> has two thousands to spend, yet if thou has no calling, tending
> to publique good, thou art an uncleane beast.[5]

The term "publique good" in this quotation is highly significant. It indicates that our Puritan forefathers valued work not for what it did for the individual but for what it contributed to the welfare of the community. The needs and interests of the individual in the seventeenth century, unlike today, were subordinated to those of the commonwealth. Not until Benjamin Franklin's time was the value of the work ethic viewed from the individual rather than the societal vantage point.

Not only were Christians to have an occupational calling but they were to pursue it with the fanatical zeal of a medieval crusader. Anything less than near total commitment to one's work denoted spiritual backsliding and invited recriminations from ministers and magistrates. Diligence in a particular calling not only adduced proof of salvation (which was indispensable for voting) but it also glorified God, and this was regarded as the chief end of man. John Robinson, who has been designated the "spiritual father of Plymouth Colony" in a recent study, solemnly asserted:

> God . . . would have no member of any societie, or body
> of men ordinarily unimployed. Neyther doth that man keep
> a good conscience before God, who makes labor but an
> accessorie, and not a principall, and that which takes up his
> ordinarie time.[6]

The inextricable connection between the calling, salvation, and voting provided a powerful mechanism for social control. Nonconformity and deviant behavior were, theoretically at least, curtailed as man channeled his energies into socially beneficial activities, thereby saving himself and his community. When the Puritan theological system began to break down with the Half-Way Covenant of 1662, the bonds of social cohesion also gave way. As a result, the work ethic became secularized and individualized, hence ideally suited to the emerging capitalistic economy.

Whereas assiduous work habits were praised by the Puritans, not surprisingly indolent behavior was denounced. Not only did idleness

lead to poverty but, worst of all, it made men more susceptible
to the temptations of the Devil. John Robinson admonished Puritans
about the "legion of vices . . . , vanities, and sinful lusts" that easily
consumed men with nothing to do. When these admonitions were
not heeded, the enforcement of vagrancy laws served as a corrective.
To forestall the evil that attended leisure time Christians were urged
to engage in moderate recreation or "seasonal merriment." [7] "We daily
need some respite & diversion, without which we dull our Powers,"
counseled Benjamin Colman in his treatise on *The Government and
Improvement of Mirth* (1707).[8]

The Puritans' major criticism of immoderate recreation was that
it failed to refresh the individual and did not enable him to pursue
his calling with renewed vigor. For this reason John Winthrop decided to give up the sport of shooting. Not only was it costly,
exhausting, and time consuming but, as he candidly confessed, he
seldom hit anything anyway. In short, hunting did not recreate or
rejuvenate his spirits. Professor Edmund S. Morgan was no doubt
correct in affirming that

> . . . no Puritan objected to recreation as such; indeed it was
> necessary for a man to indulge in frivolous pleasures from
> time to time, in order that he might return to his work re-
> freshed. But to serve the purpose, recreation had to be fun
> and not exhaust a man physically, or bore him or frustrate
> him.[9]

In contrast to the thinking of the ancient Greeks and Romans, the
New England Puritans insisted that leisure time was not to be regarded as an end in itself. [10] "Seasonal merriment" was only a means
to an end and that end was greater productivity. Improvident use
of spare time led to indolence, intemperance, and exhaustion. Those
hours that were not devoted to work were to be utilized for the
restoration of vitality, thereby allowing a man to resume his labors
with energy and resolution.

The Puritan work ethic, then, constituted several elements. Foremost was the notion of a vocational calling emanating from God.
Two corollaries of this idea were that members of the elect would
perform their calling with the utmost diligence, keeping the welfare
of the community in mind, and that time away from one's work
should be used to restore expended energy. A secularized version

of the work ethic has survived well into the twentieth century, where it has encountered highly advanced technological processes that undermine traditional assumptions about labor and leisure. The role and value of work are being scrutinized painfully by Americans who, unlike their Puritan forefathers of a bygone agrarian age, are living in a postindustrial era characterized by economic abundance and technological unemployment.

During the latter half of the nineteenth century America entered the machine age. Farming, manufacturing, and transportation became highly mechanized. Shortly after the turn of the century scientific management and assembly-line techniques gave an added boost to production and imposed new conditions and requirements on labor. Although the production of goods and services has increased by quantum leaps since the Civil War, the number of human working hours required to sustain this prodigious output has continually declined.[11] At the present time the American labor force is putting in half the number of working hours it did in the mid-nineteenth century and reaping far greater financial rewards. In 1960 the private national income was 31 times what it had been in 1850.[12] The historical trend is unmistakable. Advances in productivity have brought about an unprecedented standard of living coupled with an ever-increasing amount of leisure time.

With the advent of automation and cybernation in the years following World War II, there is every reason to believe that Americans are destined for even greater productivity and fewer working hours in the near future. Some social scientists are projecting a standard 28-to-30-hour work week accompanied by sabbatical leaves and early retirement programs.[13] The technological base of leisure will inevitably expand as man learns to harness solar power and as sophisticated electronic computers take over a larger share of routine white-collar jobs. Simultaneously, technology will provide more free time by reducing the number of hours presently devoted to sleep. Russian scientists have reportedly invented a new machine, called the "electrosone," which enables an individual to enjoy a full night of restful sleep in two hours or less. The question is not whether mass leisure is a distinct possibility. Rather it is how are Americans, imbued with a Puritan ethic, going to cope with their free time when the work-leisure tandem is reversed.

The crux of the leisure problem is not simply the task of providing enough bread and circuses to satisfy a sedentary nation. If most Americans no longer are laboring to glorify God, there are many who work, in part, to achieve a sense of identity and self-worth, as well as to gain socioeconomic status.[14] Because of Puritanism, the frontier movement, geographical mobility, and status anxieties emanating from a fluid social structure, Americans have traditionally regarded work as a way of life. Out of the crucible of America's past was forged a national temperament that to this day looks with suspicion and disfavor on able-bodied adults who do not work for a living. Praising the new "work-for-your-welfare" program in California, Governor Ronald Reagan confidently announced that it would "reintroduce the principle of the work ethic in our way of life." [15] And, contrary to popular opinion, not all members of the "Now Generation" have been able to escape the Puritan tradition, as the following remark from Hollywood activist Jane Fonda plaintively suggests:

> I've always had such miserable guilt feelings when I took a day off. It's that damned Pilgrim ethic I was brought up in. Work, work, work. Do you believe I'd shake just thinking about taking a vacation? [16]

Many of our most admired citizens are notoriously compulsive workers. In a recent opinion survey taken among Antioch College freshmen consumer-advocate Ralph Nader, who often works 20 hours a day, was selected as one of the twentieth century's leading figures.[17] Because work is still laden with such profound psychological meaning in our culture, automation is forcing many Americans into a situation they are largely unprepared to cope with. Many people would rather "moonlight," i.e., acquire a second job, than be frustrated by having uncommitted time on their hands. Herman Kahn, director of the Hudson Institute and former Rand Corporation analyst, poignantly described the leisure problem to a panel of social scientists:

> The United States is a vocation-oriented society; leisure could be catastrophic for us. The American with leisure is a man at loose ends; it will take him a generation longer to adjust to leisure than it takes the European.[18]

A more distressed outlook on this matter was registered by Alexander R. Martin, Chairman of the American Psychiatric Association's Committee on Leisure Time and Its Use:

> Symptoms of individual maladaption are: excessive guilt, compulsive behavior (especially compulsive work), increase in anxiety, depression, psychosomatic symptoms and suicide. We must face the fact that a great majority of our people are not emotionally and psychologically ready for free time. This results in unhealthy adaptations which find expression in a wide range of sociopathologic and psychopathologic states. Among the social symptoms of this maladaption to free time are: low morale, civilian unrest, subversiveness and rebellion.[19]

When these baneful effects are coupled with a crime rate that is increasing five times faster than the growth of population, one wonders, with considerable trepidation, how much longer our society can resist the Orwellian prescriptions of social engineers like Cal Tech's Robert Sinsheiner and Harvard's B. F. Skinner.[20] Our behavioral scientists, like the Puritan oligarchs before them, are dealing with the problem of American individualism in a manner that augurs the curtailment of our traditional civil liberties. Significantly, many of today's college students who find Puritanism so objectionable have not directly confronted the problem of unbridled individualism. Failure to do so may have the unfortunate effect of defaulting to the behavioral programmers.

In sum, before Americans can learn to appreciate and use their leisure time creatively they will have to revise their Puritanical conception of work. In addition, they may be forced to give serious consideration to a guaranteed annual income designed to support those who are permanently automated out of jobs.[21] For this nation such an assignment is tantamount to re-examining the purpose for living. While Americans struggle with this formidable task technological innovations will render other aspects of the traditional moral code increasingly irrelevant. The new morality, or situation ethics, will offer little solace to the troubled consciences of people who once thought they knew the difference between right and wrong. Before we can properly gauge the disparity between the old and new morality we must sketch the broad outlines of the Puritan social ethic.

Seventeenth-century New Englanders regarded order as the fundamental characteristic of God and His Creation. If order was their sheet anchor, then authority was the ballast that kept the ship of state aright and on course for the Promised Land. John Norton, a prominent Boston clergyman, underscored this view:

> Take away . . . order, and how shall peace, or the society continue? This truth of a magisterial judge is reckoned among the Fundamentals . . . if it be in matters of religion, there is the Priest; if in matters civil, there is the Magistrate, and he that stands not, or submits not to the sentence of these, let him be cast out from Israel: so requisite a thing is order. [22]

Order, then, was the touchstone of the Puritan cosmology. From this original premise concerning the nature of God and the universe was deduced a categorical and prescriptive moral code that correlated with the Bible.

While the Antinomian controversy rocked the foundations of the Bay Colony in January 1636, another ominous event occurred. John Winthrop and Thomas Dudley engaged in a feud over the administration of justice in Massachusetts Bay. Governor Winthrop argued in favor of establishing a somewhat lenient juridical code because of the unsettled conditions in the colony. He urged that discipline should be tempered according to the nature of the situation or circumstance. Dudley, who was more of a Philistine by disposition, persuaded the oligarchy to adopt a strict and inflexible code of justice. This decision reflected sheer moral and legal absolutism. Discipline could not be adjusted to accommodate changing or exceptional circumstances; instead, it "must remain fixed and ultimate to protect the universal law of morality, the honor and safety of the gospel." [23] God's immutable laws had been indelibly inscribed on the Tablets of Stone for all men and all times. Cotton Mather later summed up Dudley's position quite appropriately when he stated: "Crook not God's rules to the experience of men, but bring them unto the rule, and try men's estates herein by that." [24] Naturally, the "rule" that Mather referred to was the inviolable Word of God. The Scriptures alone contained the just and fixed laws applicable to every possible contingency and misdeed.

As long as America remained predominantly rural, agrarian, and Yankee, the Puritan social ethic gave meaning and direction to peoples' lives. If Wax Weber exaggerated in asserting that the Protestant ethic gave rise to the spirit of capitalism, there were many points at which the two forces were mutually supportive. But during the early twentieth century this symbiotic relationship between the Puritan ethic and commercial society began to break down. At the time of the Progressive movement Americans were exposed to the problem of ethical confusion that resulted from the "attempt to apply the moral code of an individualistic agrarian society to the practices of a highly industrialized and integrated social order." [25]

When World War II was brought to a close, America entered a transitional stage between the industrial and technetronic eras. The impact of science and technology further aggravated the prevailing confusion in American values. Our once clearly defined roles of the family, work, and the sexes became increasingly blurred. According to Columbia's Zbigniew Brzezinski,

> ... In the emerging technetronic society automation threatens both males and females, intellectual talent is computable, the "pill" encourages sexual equality, and women begin to claim complete equality. [26]

The absolute and well-defined tenets of the traditional Puritan ethic have outlived the earlier age for which their relevance seemed most obvious.[27] For nearly a generation Americans have been searching for a viable moral code that is relevant to the new age of industrial and biological technology. A young Radcliffe coed put the matter succinctly when she told a Los Angeles Times editor that "people are groping desperately for some personal code of ethics. There isn't any good guiding principle to follow now." [28] In the late 1950s the dim outlines of a new ethic could be discerned.

As a method of arriving at moral decisions, situation ethics marks a departure from the traditional legalistic and prescriptive approach of the New England Puritans. Eschewing the alleged simplicity, inflexibility, and injustice connected with moral absolutism, situation ethicist Joseph Fletcher argues that under the new morality "anything and everything is right or wrong, according to the situation."[29]

For the Christian situation ethicist the only fixed standard to be applied to every moral problem is the law of agapeic love.[30] For the non-Christian situation ethicist some other *summum bonum*, such as Aristotle's principle of self-realization, will serve as the only absolute ethical standard. This does not mean that the moral wisdom of past ages is necessarily discarded to make way for the new hedonism. The contextual approach is not to be confused with Antinomianism. Under situation ethics the ancient moral precepts are regarded as maxims rather than laws. These ethical guidelines are not to be slavishly followed when they conflict with the serving of some ultimate good.[31]

Although the Puritanical and contextual approaches to morality could be contrasted in many areas, much of the present controversy has centered on their respective postures toward the changing norms of sexual conduct. Perhaps an application of the two ethical approaches to the matter of sexual behavior will exemplify the distinctive features of each.

Any assessment of the sexual mores of colonial New England must be divested of the hoary myth that Puritans were monastic kill-joys. After searching through tomes of church sermons and court cases, Yale historian Edmund S. Morgan persuasively concludes that they "possessed a high degree of virility and very few inhibitions."[32] Sexual relations between men and women were governed by two absolute prohibitions: sexual activity between unmarried persons was unlawful and intercourse between married persons was never to interfere with religion. Perhaps because of their acute awareness of man's physical appetites, Puritan authorities frequently mitigated the penalties that were meted out to sexual offenders; for example, adultery was a capital crime in Massachusetts Bay (unlike Plymouth Colony), but in only three known instances was the death penalty invoked for convicted adulterers.[33] Although the colonists of New England would not bend or reduce their high sexual standards, they made allowances for man's libidinous drives by encouraging early marriages and by tempering the enforcement of their laws. Absolute restrictions, then, were few and their violation by wayward Puritans seldom exacted the full measure of the law.

The underlying reasons for their sexual prohibitions are not difficult to find. Cases of fornication and adultery were so numerous in seventeenth-century New England that the problem of caring for illegitimate children imposed an onerous financial burden on the commonwealth. Also, sex outside nuptial bonds struck at the foundations of the family and therefore loosened the linchpin of social order and economic well-being. Furthermore, because man's ultimate purpose was to glorify God, any activity that interfered with the spiritual life was to be curtailed.

Although some of these reasons for restricting sexual activity may no longer seem compelling, the old Puritan morality has not disappeared. In 1959 the California State Subcommittee on Pornographic Literature issued a report echoing the strictures of the Bay Colony ministers:

> We believe it to be a principle of our Nation that premarital or extramarital sexual activity is dangerous and unhealthy. Anything that incites or lures or glorifies such activity is objectionable.[34]

Aaron Stern, a psychoanalyst who oversees the rating guidelines of the Motion Picture Association of America, recently complained about the Puritanic legacy that continues to inhibit Americans:

> Our Puritan fathers set up the groundwork for a social system anchored in a distorted conviction relative to man's inherent evil. . . . They contributed to the construction of the American ideal in terms of the New England tradition of a disciplined, dutiful, responsible and frequently sterile individual who stringently policed any overt expression of [sexual] feelings. But their prejudice should not become a yardstick to govern all of us who have followed in their wake.[35]

As founder and head of the $127-million-a-year Playboy empire, Hugh M. Hefner has amassed a fortune debunking and counteracting the *bête noire* of American culture—the "puritanism [which] pervades every aspect of our lives." [36]

Biological technology, especially in the area of birth control, has been largely responsible for the current revision of America's sexual mores. Unwanted and unplanned pregnancies can now be prevented by oral contraceptives and intrauterine devices. The development and utilization of potent antibiotics like penicillin has reduced the risk of of venereal disease for those who are inclined to have multiple sexual encounters. Liberalized state abortion laws and improved techniques of aborting, such as the amniocentesis procedure, have released numerous women from involuntary childbirth. Joseph Fletcher, Professor of Medical Ethics at the University of Virginia School of Medicine, clearly recognized the relationship between the new biological technology and America's changing sexual norms when he observed:

> The triple terrors of infection, conception, and detection which once scared people into "Christian" sex relations (marital monopoly) have pretty well become obsolete through medicine.[37]

With the old perils of infectious disease and unwanted childbirth greatly diminished by modern medical science the way has been paved for liberalized sexual standards.

Under situation ethics there is nothing intrinsically wrong with either premarital sex or adultery. The context of a particular act determines whether one has behaved in a moral or immoral fashion. If a person is exploited or injured, then agapeic love has not been served and the act can be considered immoral. There may, however, be instances in which sexual relations outside of wedlock can be regarded as morally right; for example, situation ethicists sometimes cite the case of Mrs. Bergmeier who, while foraging for her three children in wartorn Germany, was seized by a Soviet patrol and sent off to a Russian prison camp in the Ukraine.[38] After receiving news that her husband and children were alive in Berlin but perilously near starvation she became determined to rejoin her beleaguered family. Cognizant of a prison ordinance that required the immediate release of pregnant women, she had sexual relations with an obliging guard, became expectant, and was allowed to return to her family. The situation ethicist would conclude that her act of sacrificial adultery, which was impelled by the highest of motives, was moral and justifiable.

In the foregoing pages the origins and nature of America's ethical predicament have been studied. It has been shown that the traditional

Puritan ethic encountered automation and the new morality midway through the twentieth century and that American values have been in a state of profound confusion ever since. Frustrated by the reduced work week, compulsory leisure, and the erosion of traditional morality, many older people yearn nostalgically for a return to the halcyon years of America's past. Younger generations find themselves uncongenially situated between the Scylla of Establishment Puritanism and the Charybdis of Hugh Hefner's playboy philosophy. The middle way, situation ethics, imposes a rigorous calculus of priorities without offering the certainty and assurance of the old standards.

Underlying the transformation of America's values have been the changing forms of technology. Just as the landed frontier once played an instrumental role in shaping American history, today it is the technological frontier that foreshadows the course of our development. It is nearly impossible to evaluate, much less anticipate, the impact of technology on American life until we adequately appraise the influence of our Puritan past. Then we shall know why it will take the American a generation longer than the European to adjust to leisure. Twentieth-century technology, like nineteenth-century free land, has had a differential impact on nations throughout the world. Each industrially mature country has had to adjust its cultural values to the new problems and prospects of the technetronic era. Perhaps Harry Haller's disconsolate search for identity and a sense of equilibrium is the unavoidable plight of people living in scientifically advanced nations, but in America the trauma produced by rapid change may be less painful when we understand how the traditional Puritan ethic conditions our response to the new technological age.

Notes

1. Alvin Toffler, *Future Shock* (New York: Bantam, 1971), p. 2.
2. Kai T. Erikson, *Wayward Puritans: A Study in the Sociology of Deviance* (New York: Wiley, 1966), p. 189.
3. Gilman M. Ostrander, *American Civilization in the First Machine Age, 1890–1940* (New York: Harper & Row, 1970), p. 239.
4. William Perkins, *A Treatise of the Vocations or Callings of Men* (1608), cited by Stephen Foster, *Their Solitary Way: The Puritan Social Ethic in*

the First Century of Settlement in New England (New Haven: Yale University Press, 1971), p. 99.

5. John Cotton, *The Way of Life* (1641), cited by Foster, *Their Solitary Way,* ˙ p. 100.

6. John Robinson, "Diligent Labor and the Use of God's Creature," from *Observations of Knowledge and Virtue* (1625), cited by Richard Reinitz, Ed., *Tensions in American Puritanism* (New York: Wiley, 1970), p. 66.

7. Robert Lee, *Religion and Leisure in America: A Study in Four Dimensions* (New York: Abingdon, 1964), p. 159. See Chapter 8 for a thorough and scholarly account of Puritan attitudes toward work and leisure.

8. Cited by Perry Miller and Thomas H. Johnson, Eds., *The Puritans: A Sourcebook of Their Writings* (New York: Harper & Row, 1963), II, p. 392.

9. Edmund S. Morgan, *The Puritan Dilemma: The Story of John Winthrop* (Boston: Little, Brown, 1958), p. 10.

10. The ancient Greek and Roman philosophers regarded leisure as the hallmark of an advanced culture. Socrates reportedly stated that leisure was "the best of all possessions," but Aristotle was the one who frequently used the term *scholē*, meaning to halt or cease, which is the etymological root of the word "leisure." Aristotle equated *scholē* with peace, happiness, and the pursuit of wisdom. In the *Ethics* he carefully distinguished between amusement (*paidia*), recreation (*anapausis*), and leisure (*scholē*). The first two were necessary because of work; that is, they enabled one to resume his occupation with renewed industry. Amusement and recreation were not ultimate goals. "Leisure is a different matter," observed Aristotle. "We think of it as having in itself intrinsic pleasure, intrinsic happiness, intrinsic felicity. Happiness of that order does not belong to occupation; it belongs to those who have leisure." For a thorough discussion of this matter, see Chapter 1 of Sebastian de Grazia's *Of Time, Work, and Leisure* (New York: The Twentieth Century Fund, 1962). An incisive critique of the classical view of leisure appears in Lee, *Religion and Leisure in America*, pp. 33–35.

11. "Estimated Average Weekly Work Hours: 1850–1960," extracted from J. Frederic Dewhurst and Associates, *America's Needs and Resources: A New Survey* (New York: The Twentieth Century Fund, 1955), Appendix 20-4, p. 1073.

1850	69.8	1910	55.1
1860	68.0	1920	49.7
1870	65.4	1930	45.0
1880	64.0	1940	44.0
1890	61.9	1950	40.0
1900	60.0	1960	37.5

12. Max Kaplan, *Leisure in America: A Social Inquiry* (New York: Wiley, 1960), p. 35. Professor Kaplan imaginatively illustrates this point by suggesting that "each of us has at our daily disposal as much power—as many services—as would in the preindustrial days have required 90 slaves." (p. 36)

13. James C. Charlesworth, Ed., *Leisure in America: Blessing or Curse* (Philadelphia: The American Academy of Political and Social Science, 1964), p. 12; Daniel Bell, Ed., *Toward the Year 2000: Work in Progress* (Boston: Beacon, 1968), p. 331.

14. Lee Taylor, *Occupational Sociology* (New York: Oxford University Press, 1968), pp. 399–401; Michael Harrington, *The Accidental Century* (New York: Macmillan, 1965), p. 257; Arthur M. Schlesinger, "Our New-Found Leisure Won't Bore Us if Some of It Is Employed in Reading," *The Saturday Evening Post* (April 18, 1959), 10.

15. *Los Angeles Times,* March 4, 1972, p. 25.

16. *Ibid., West* Magazine, insert (March 21, 1971), 18.

17. *The National Observer,* January 15, 1972, p. 6. Ralph Nader's Puritanic work habits and ascetic life style would have been exemplary even in seventeenth-century New England. Earning more than $100,000 a year from honorariums alone, he lives on less than $5000 in one room of a boarding house without a car or television set. The remainder of his income is reportedly channeled into his investigations. See *Time* (May 10, 1971), 18. Nader's addiction to work was discussed in an editorial appearing in the Opinion Section of the *Los Angeles Times,* March 26, 1972, p. 6. The writer of that editorial culled a revealing anecdote from Charles McCarry's book, *Citizen Nader:* "When Jacobs (Ted Jacobs, a Nader aide) and his wife took a summer house at the beach, Nader asked with genuine curiosity what they did when they went there. 'Oh, we lie on the beach, we read the papers, and we go for walks, we have lunch on the porch,' Jacobs replied. Nader said, 'That takes all weekend?' "

18. Bell, *Toward the Year 2000,* p. 331. See also De Grazia, *Of Time, Work, and Leisure,* pp. 46–51.

19. Charles R. Dechert, Ed., *The Social Impact of Cybernation* (Notre Dame, Indiana: University of Notre Dame Press, 1966), pp. 55–56.

20. See the interview with B. F. Skinner entitled "I Have Been Misunderstood" appearing in *The Center Magazine* (March/April 1972), 63–65; Joseph Wood Krutch, "What the Year 2000 Won't Be Like," *Saturday Review* (January 20, 1968), 12–14, 43.

21. Robert Theobald, "Should Men Compete with Machines?" *The Nation* (May 9, 1966), 546.

22. John Norton, *Sion the out-cast healed of her Wounds* (1664), cited by Foster, *Their Solitary Way,* p. 21.

23. Erikson, *Wayward Puritans,* p. 187.

24. Miller, *The New England Mind: The Seventeenth Century* (Boston: Beacon, 1968), p. 20.

25. Samuel Eliot Morison, Henry Steele Commager, and William E. Leuchtenburg, *The Growth of the American Republic,* 6th ed. (New York: Oxford University Press, 1969), II, p. 268.

26. Zbigniew Brzezinski, *Between Two Ages: America's Role in the Technetronic Era* (New York: Viking, 1970), p. 13.
27. Elting E. Morison, Ed., *The American Style: Essays in Value and Performance* (New York: Harper, 1958), pp. 145–217.
28. *Los Angeles Times,* Opinion Section, February 20, 1972, p. 7.
29. Joseph Fletcher, *Situation Ethics: The New Morality* (Philadelphia: Westminster, 1966), p. 124.
30. Agapeic love is oftentimes nonreciprocal and is extended to one's neighbors as well as enemies. It is distinguished from friendship love (*philia*) and romantic love (*erōs*), both of which are selective. Also erotic and philic love are emotional, whereas agapeic love is more of an attitude than a feeling. See Fletcher, *Situation Ethics,* p. 79.
31. For a traditionalist's rejoinder see Arnold W. Green, "The New Morality," *Modern Age: A Quarterly Review* (Summer-Fall, 1970), 293–304.
32. Edmund S. Morgan, "The Puritans and Sex," *The New England Quarterly* (December 1942), 596.
33. *Ibid.,* p. 602.
34. California, Assembly, Committee on Judiciary, *Report of the Subcommittee on Pornographic Literature,* on H. R. 224, 1959, p. 10.
35. *Los Angeles Times, West* Magazine insert (July 16, 1972), 22–23.
36. Hugh M. Hefner, "The Playboy Philosophy," *Playboy* (July 1963), 45. See also Digby Diehl's interview with Hefner appearing in the *Los Angeles Times, West* Magazine insert (February 27, 1972), 20–23.
37. Fletcher, *Situation Ethics,* p. 80.
38. *Ibid.,* pp. 165–65.

FROM ONE . . .

Puritanism in Old and New England was a dangerous force for
any political regime that confronted it. As Professor Michael
Walzer points out in *The Revolution of the Saints,* the Puritan
was the first "active, ideologically committed radical" in modern
history. A deep sense of religious commitment, coupled with
Spartan discipline, enabled God's elect to wage effective warfare
against their worldly foes. Revolution against a despotic and
sinful government was not merely a right but a duty sanctioned
by God. "No civil rulers are to be obeyed when they enjoin things
that are inconsistent with the commands of God," asserted
Boston Minister Jonathan Mayhew in 1750. A secularized version
of the Puritan revolutionary credo spilled over into the eighteenth century and was instrumental in sparking the War for
Independence. A comparative view of "The American Revolution and the New Radicalism" may help us to draw appropriate
conclusions about the right of revolution today.

. . . ON TO TWO

We must realize that today's Establishment is the new George III. Whether it will continue to adhere to his tactics, we do not know. If it does, the redress, honored in tradition, is also revolution.

Justice William O. Douglas (1969)

TWO

THE AMERICAN REVOLUTION AND THE NEW RADICALISM

THOMAS J. OSBORNE

On a sweltering and humid afternoon in mid-August 1966 the House Un-American Activities Committee conducted hearings on a newly proposed conspiracy measure. It had been drafted largely in response to recent antiwar disturbances in Berkeley, California. The ill-planned hearings, which took place in an overcrowded chamber, quickly deteriorated into a disorderly array of undignified exchanges between Congressmen and Vietnam War protesters. No sooner had the proceedings begun than the haunting specter of the American Revolution set the tone for the drama that was about to unfold.

In the midst of clamor and confusion Attorney Alfred M. Nittle, counsel for the H.U.A.C., ordered one protester to identify himself and state his views on the Vietnam War. "I will state that the U.S. is the aggressor in Vietnam. I am Jeffrey Gordon and I identify with the American Revolution," retorted the witness.[1] On hearing this, Congressman Joe R. Pool, a Texas Democrat who chaired the examining subcommittee, rejoined sarcastically: "I know another man who identified with the American Revolution. I think his first name was Benedict." This pungent remark was greeted with applause and epithets. Meanwhile, Jerry Clyde Rubin, an organizer of the Vietnam Day Committee in Berkeley, was busily handing out parchment reproductions of the Declaration of Independence. A reporter from *The New York Times* observed Rubin wearing "a handlebar mustache and a Revolutionary War uniform with tails, gold buttons, and a tricorn hat."[2] The radical leader exclaimed that his costume and literature symbolized "the fact that America was born in a revolution." By attempting to throttle resistance to the Vietnam War our government was "denying the right of others to revolution," inveighed Rubin. In this dramatic and obtrusive manner the young dissidents invoked America's revolutionary heritage to justify the allegedly rebellious conduct of the war protesters.

These angry young men were doing what a generation of historians and statesmen have neglected to do: they were applying America's revolutionary past to our nation's disorderly present. Since the end of World War II the tendency has been for the American historical guild to extol the virtues of 1776 and offer its principles and hopes to the colonized nations of the world. The writings of the late Arthur M. Schlesinger and Richard B. Morris afford two excellent examples of this kind of scholarship. In the March 1959 issue of *The Atlantic* Professor Schlesinger asserted that America's foremost gift to civilization was "the inherent and universal right of revolution proclaimed in the Declaration of Independence."[3] He then proceeded to demonstrate how our revolution influenced subsequent eruptions in Europe and South America. A more recent study by the eminent Richard B. Morris proposes that the American Revolution continue to serve as a model for the emerging nations in Africa and Asia.[4]

Our political leaders have taken much the same tack as the historians. When the late President John F. Kennedy launched the Alliance for Progress in 1961, he eloquently stated:

> Across vast turbulent continents these American ideals will
> stir Man's struggle for national independence and individual
> freedom. But, as we welcome the spread of the American
> Revolution to other lands we must also remember that our
> hemisphere's mission is not yet complete. . . . Let us again
> awaken our American Revolution until it guides the struggle
> of people everywhere.[5]

The clear implication of Kennedy's speech seems to be that the
American Revolution is for "export only." Ten years later President
Richard M. Nixon addressed the American people on Independence
Day and reminded them that "the future peace of the world is in
our hands."[6] Kennedy stressed world freedom; Nixon focused on
world peace. Neither of them effectively related 1776 to current
domestic politics.

If today's militants accomplish nothing else, they may force scholars, politicians, students, and laymen to examine the relevance of
1776 to contemporary American society. The search for this kind
of meaning should become widespread as the bicentennial anniversary
approaches us. It seems paradoxical that the nation that sent the
revolutionary snowball tumbling on its downhill course in 1776 should
have so much difficulty gauging its path and velocity 200 years later.
America proudly spawned the "age of democratic revolutions" but
has failed or been unwilling to contemplate what may be the broader
implications of that fateful act. The paradox assumes even greater
proportions when we consider that the radicals subpoenaed before
the H.U.A.C. may have conducted themselves in accordance with
the nation's most exemplary tradition while the interrogating subcommittee may have been the party guilty of committing un-
American acts.

Having defined the problem and being mindful of its complexities
and seeming paradoxes, we can now attempt to shed some light
on the "relevance of 1776 to contemporary American society."
Chronological as well as topical considerations suggest focusing first
on the theory that justifies the American Revolution and second
on the nature of that upheaval. In this manner the War for Independence can be studied and linked to the new radical movement.

The Declaration of Independence contains, perhaps, history's most
famous and eloquent statement of the revolutionary ideology. In the
ominous and felicitous passages of that document Thomas Jefferson

deduced the right of revolution from a theoretical body of natural and inalienable rights. One of the most coveted among them is the right to self-government; that is, all government is based on the voluntary consent of the people. When the existing government no longer secured those ends for which it was formed, namely, the safety and happiness of its citizens, the latter retained the right to withdraw their consent and "alter or abolish" the existing regime.

But the natural and inalienable right of revolution was by no means unconditional. Jefferson believed that only under certain circumstances was this right to be exercised. The forceful overthrow of an existing government should never occur for "light and transient" reasons and should follow only on a "long train of abuses and usurpations." John Locke, whom Jefferson unconsciously plagiarized, "was vehement in his condemnation of individuals who would foment revolution against a just government."[7] Aggravations and corruption would attend any political system. Experience had shown that it was better for mankind to endure them patiently rather than to revolt, and as long as legal channels remained open, enabling peaceful revolution, there could be no recourse to forceful overthrow of the government. Even when repeated injuries were inflicted and the legal channels clogged, it still had to be shown that the transgressions were calculated to wrest power and liberty from the people. The Declaration's blanket indictment against George III was written to impugn the motives as well as the conduct of the Hanoverian King.[8]

Furthermore, suicidal rebellions such as the Watts riots of 1965 were clearly outside the pale of the natural rights ideology. Uprisings that were actively supported by only a handful of the people and had no hope of success violated the original right of nature—the right (indeed the duty) to preserve one's life.

Nearly all the revolutionary leaders, from John Adams to Thomas Paine, recognized property ownership as a basic natural right. Although the Declaration does not specifically assign governments the responsibility of protecting private property, the Founders were nevertheless convinced that this was one of those ends for which governments were created. In describing the duties of governments, Jefferson merely substituted the phrase "pursuit of happiness" for Locke's emphasis on the word "property." The two terms were nearly interchangeable, for, in most instances, one's happiness is directly proportional to the amount of anxiety he suffers with respect to the security of his belongings. The point of this matter is that the Declaration nowhere denies the right to own or acquire property. Instead, this right was implicitly recognized.[9] In this sense the theory justifying the American Revolution was distinctly conservative.

In sum, revolution was a very grave matter. In legitimizing it, the Founding Fathers were not seeking to destroy political authority in general, nor were they attacking the principle of private property. They were only undermining British sovereignty over the 13 colonies. Even before this theory of revolution was proclaimed it was necessary to prove that a despotism of great magnitude was being imposed on the people for the express purpose of reducing them to vassalage.

Many of today's political activists look to the Declaration of Independence as their ideological touchstone. Like most extremist groups, the New Left is composed of those who are cerebrally motivated and others who are more responsive to visceral stimuli. The radical intelligentsia form a coterie of articulate professionals and scholars. Allowing for varying shades of opinion and commitment, their high priests include historian Staughton Lynd, Supreme Court Justice William O. Douglas, defense attorney William M. Kunstler, sociologist C. Wright Mills, and philosopher Herbert Marcuse. Not surprisingly, it has been the head of this new body, more so than the hands, that has attempted to rationalize cataclysmic change in accordance with the principles of 1776.

New Left historian Staughton Lynd asserts, with perhaps a great deal of truth, that "for almost two hundred years all kinds of American radicals have traced their intellectual origins to the Declaration of Independence and to the revolution it justified."[10] In other words, continued Lynd, there is "an unbroken continuity between the revolutionaries of 1776 and twentieth-century radicals." The appropriateness of Lockean natural rights doctrine for today's radical movement seemed quite apparent to Professor Lynd, who states:

> Distant and archaic as it may often appear, the language of the Declaration of Independence remains relevant as an instrument for social transformation. . . . Men should be free,

according to the revolutionary tradition, because on joining
society they do not surrender their essential powers. If existing
society abuses those powers, men should demand their restoration at once.[11]

It should be noted that although Staughton Lynd defends the right
of revolution and even though he has flagrantly violated federal law
(by making an unauthorized visit to North Vietnam in 1965) he has
been careful not to advocate publicly the violent overthrow of the
government.[12]

A recent issue of the *National Review* denounced Supreme Court
Justice William O. Douglas for being a member of the "Kunstler
Constituency" of revolutionaries.[13] Whether Douglas advocates the
overthrow of our government seems uncertain. The issue is charged
with a great deal of controversy.[14] That he defends the right to
do so, however, is indisputable. The "enduring appeal" of the Declaration of Independence, wrote Douglas, was that it crystallized the
principle "that revolution can be a righteous course, that the throwing
off of chains by an oppressed people is a noble project." [15] In his
recent book, entitled *Points of Rebellion*, he issues a somber
warning to the American people. Unless the Establishment, which
Douglas equates with George III, spearheads an "explosive political
regeneration," America will undergo a violent revolution similar to
1776.[16] The historical analogy is ominous and unmistakable.

On earning Phi Beta Kappa honors at Yale and graduating from
Columbia Law School, William Moses Kunstler seemed an unlikely
prospect to become "America's most controversial and, perhaps, best
known lawyer." [17] Like the changing color tones of the proverbial
chameleon, the political views of this former Macy's executive trainee
have taken on an increasingly radical complexion. With obvious
reference to the 1770s, Kunstler addressed 350 angry young listeners
at Columbia University:

We have a duty to do more than protest illegitimate authority.
There apparently is not going to be an ear to listen to our
protest. Therefore, we must turn to other forms. . . . Why
was it perfectly honorable to drop 342 bags of tea in Boston
Harbor? When John Adams heard about it, he said 'I would
as lief it had been 342 British carcasses floating in the harbor.'
This from our 'non-violent forefathers'.[18]

One week later this intransigent lawyer addressed a throng of 25,000 demonstrators in New York's Bryant Park. After delivering his usual harangue about the Establishment's repression of dissenters, he exhorted the crowd to go into the streets and do "everything short of revolution." [19] A reporter from *The New York Times* noted that Kunstler cited "William O. Douglas of the Supreme Court as his authority for the view that even revolution might become necessary." [20] Like Staughton Lynd and William O. Douglas, this self-styled Patrick Henry of the New Left was using the men and principles of 1776 to vindicate the unlawful acts of the new revolutionaries.

Compared with some of the clever historical analogies drawn by the radical intelligentsia, the attempts of militants to rationalize revolution are palpably feeble. Their rhetoric betrays nearly every tenet of the Declaration's revolutionary creed. In stark contrast to Jefferson's forebodings against revolution for "light and transient" reasons Yippie leader Abbie Hoffman fatuously enjoins his followers to embark on "revolution for the hell of it." [21] Anticipating the hedonistic joys that attend violent disruption, Jerry Rubin is convinced that "it's gotta be more fun to be in the revolution than out of it." [22] During the campus unrest at U.C.L.A. in the spring of 1970 the *Daily Bruin* quoted Rubin as shouting, "to me, a riot's a party." [23] Today's hard-core radicals almost uniformly rule out peaceful revolution through existing channels. Impervious to the natural law dictum against suicidal revolution, Rubin insists that "a movement [which] isn't willing to risk injuries, even deaths, isn't for ———." [24]

Furthermore, these militant leaders have no regard for the natural right of property ownership. Eldridge Cleaver, a spokesman for the Black Panthers, argues that "blacks are in no position to respect or help maintain the institution of private property." [25] After equating money with human feces in a recent publication, Rubin exclaims, "burning money and credit cards and property is an act of love, an act on behalf of humanity." [25] And Tom Hayden, former president of the Students for a Democratic Society, states that the first goal of today's revolutionaries is to "abolish a private property system which . . . benefits only a few." [27]

Although some intellectuals in the movement attempt to reconcile their revolutionary ideology with the Declaration of Independence, we find little in the way of incisive comparative analysis. Both

Professor Lynd and Justice Douglas seem to extrapolate the conditional right of revolution from the Declaration, but neither of them carefully explores the prerequisites to exercising that right. Furthermore, the leading activists are justifying revolution on grounds that are totally incongruous with that document. With little to connect the two revolutionary movements in terms of theory, perhaps we can find something about the nature of the American Revolution that could render it the archetype of today's liberation movement.

Did an internal revolution occur while the 13 colonies prosecuted the War for Independence; or, as the late Carl Becker posed this intriguing question, was the American Revolution fought to decide the issue of "who should rule at home" as well as the one of "home rule"?[28] Some historians have argued that "home rule" was the only issue, whereas others, like Becker, have maintained that a dual revolution was fought. Although this matter is complicated, it is highly pertinent. We must explore both views and their implications in order to compare the Revolution of 1776 with its modern counterpart.

During the years before World War II many historians subscribed to the notion that an intracolonial class war was generated by a propertyless proletariat in 1776. Adherents of this class-conflict thesis also maintained that America's internal convulsion ushered in sweeping democratic reforms. Recent historical scholarship tends to undermine this view.[29] Some of the postwar revisionists have pointed out that although Tory estates were confiscated it was not for the purpose of distributing real estate among landless colonials. Loyalist property was expropriated to help defray the rising costs of the war and in many instances these holdings were sold to wealthy land speculators. Furthermore, the abolition of primogeniture, entails, and quitrents during the Revolution constituted a rather hollow victory for the middle and lower classes, for these practices had been discontinued in most of the colonies before 1776. Finally, the overwhelming majority of America's 500,000 Negro slaves were just as secure in their bondage in 1783 as before the Revolution.

Although the upheaval of 1776 may not have been a social revolution, there were, as New Left historian Jesse Lemisch points out, numerous instances of mob violence and class antagonism.[30] The socioeconomic cleavage between Jack Tar and John Bull frequently

invited destructive outbursts from the mechanics of Philadelphia and
the seamen of Boston and New York. Also, it is undeniable that
the American Revolution had a democratizing effect in many of
the states.[31] All of this, however, should not obscure the fact that
the Revolution, especially in terms of its origins, was primarily a
war for independence. Although the term "revolution" was employed
by contemporaries, they were using the word in the idiom of seventeenth-century English thought to denote a "revolving back" to the
pretyrannical era of virtual self-government, that is, the period before
1763.[32] Its usage in no way implied that a social convulsion had
occurred. The confrontations that took place between 1763 and 1776
did not pit colonist against colonist but Americans against English-
men. Without the war against England there would have been no
armed conflict between Patriots and Loyalists. New Leftist Staughton
Lynd admitted this when he said, "the evidence is overwhelming
that internal conflict was a secondary aspect of the revolution of
1776, which in fact was primarily a war for national independence." [33]
The democratizing effects of the Revolution were only incidental
to it in much the same way that women's suffrage was an unintended
outgrowth of America's involvement in World War I. Professor
Richard B. Morris summed it up quite appropriately when he stated:

> We did not declare our independence of George III in order
> to reform the land laws, change the criminal codes, spread
> popular education, or separate church and state. We broke
> with England to achieve political independence . . . , but
> in the process . . . we . . . created a climate conducive to
> a measurable degree of social reform.[34]

In identifying their cause with that of the revolutionaries of 1776,
today's radicals are overlooking the point that in all likelihood no
social revolution occurred. The class antagonism and liberative cur-
rents, which in some instances characterized the American Revolution, were part of a broader reform movement that started before
1776 and spilled over into the Confederation period. Therefore, if
present-day revolutionaries, such as the Weathermen and Black
Panthers, wish to compare their movement with the American Revolution, they must find some way to identify with the war for independence that was waged against a colonizing mother country.

Kwame Nkrumah, the noted Marxist scholar and former President of Ghana, has sketched the broad outlines of an approach that may seem useful in achieving this kind of identification. In commenting on the nature of colonialism, Nkrumah states:

> A colony is any territory in which the interests of the people are alienated from them and subjected to those of a group distinct from the people of the territory itself. It follows that a colony may be externally or internally subjected. . . . When the interests [of the people] are subjected to those of a class, in the sense of Marx, within the territory itself it is said to be internally subjected.[35]

Although Nkrumah was utilizing the theory of internal colonialism to explain the apartheid arrangement in the Union of South Africa, some American radicals have been applying it to the United States.

Huey P. Newton, the Black Panther Minister of Defense, has said: "the Party's position is that the Black people in the country [America] are definitely colonized, and suffer from the colonial plight more than any ethnic group." [36] Eldridge Cleaver, the Panther's celebrated fugitive, alludes to this domestic imperialism in his book, *Soul On Ice*. After citing a quotation from Nkrumah, Cleaver proceeds to identify America's rebelling colonials as "Negroes, the aged, [the] unemployed and unemployable, the poor, the miseducated and dissatisfied students, [and] the haters of war." [37] It should be noted that the Panther's Ten Point Platform and Program quotes verbatim the Declaration's revolutionary credo as justification for launching their colonial war for independence.[38] Perhaps what makes the historical analogy with 1776 even more striking is the talk about creating a new nation—the Republic of New Africa—out of America's scattered black enclaves.

Tom Hayden, a member of the Chicago Seven and one of the country's leading revolutionaries, broadly applies the theory of internal colonialism to white communities as well as black ghettos.[39] Some of these predominantly white or mixed colonies are Berkeley, Haight-Ashbury, Isla Vista, Madison, Ann Arbor, Greenwich Village, and North Beach. According to Hayden, communes and university villages are springing up all over the United States and their young inhabitants are pursuing a way of life that is inimical and repugnant to white, middle-class Americans. Eventually these Free Territories, as Hayden refers to them, will become targets of fascist oppression.

Naturally their inhabitants will simultaneously provoke and resist outside interference. "If there is revolutionary change inside the Mother Country," wrote Hayden, "it will originate in the Berkeleys and Madisons, where people are similarly rooted and where we are defending ourselves against growing aggression." [40] Enough of these violent confrontations coupled with the growing fascism of the Washington government will trigger "The New American Revolution." [41] All of this will begin taking place in the 1970s. It is interesting to note that in Hayden's new book, entitled *Trial*, he precedes this call for revolution by quoting the following passage from the Declaration of the Causes and Necessity of Taking Up Arms (1775): "We for ten years incessantly and ineffectually besieged the throne as supplicants; we reasoned, we remonstrated with Parliament in the most mild and decent language." Not surprisingly, this citation was followed by an indictment against the federal government's allegedly futile attempts to reform the system during the 1960s. [42]

The colonial war analogy is interesting but vulnerable. It seems ludicrous to regard the domestic policies of the federal government as imperialistic. According to the *Oxford English Dictionary*, imperialism, in the American sense, refers to

> the new policy of extending the rule of the American people over foreign countries and acquiring and holding distant dependencies in the way in which colonies and dependencies are held by European states. [43]

Even if we disregard the reference to "foreign countries" and "distant dependencies," imperialism does not exist within America. In the continental United States the Constitution follows the flag. Theoretically at least, the adult inhabitants of America's revolutionary strongholds have been entitled to the same rights and privileges as all other citizens of this country. They have not, in a legal sense, been treated as a subject people. In fact, it could be argued that some campus militants have enjoyed special immunities. Even if the opposite were true and unpopular minority rights were violated, the federal government might be deemed oppressive but certainly not imperialistic. To label the domestic policies of the American government as imperialistic is to confuse the concept of imperialism with that of national sovereignty.

Furthermore, if a colony is a "settlement in a new country," then America's only domestic colonies, in a strict political sense, were those established in the seventeenth and eighteenth centuries.[44] In sum, the theory of internal colonialism was formulated by an African statesman to describe a circumstance prevailing in the Union of South Africa. The literal application of that concept to the United States tends to obfuscate rather than illuminate the nature of today's liberation movement.

In the foregoing pages the American Revolution has been examined in terms of its theoretical underpinnings and internal characteristics. The Declaration's revolutionary ideology was studied and linked to its modern exponents who seemed to disregard some of the major tenets of that doctrine. Also, it has been shown that America's eighteenth-century upheaval was primarily, but not exclusively, a colonial war for political independence. If today's militants wish to identify their movement with the American Revolution, they must keep this in mind. Employing the theory of internal colonialism to render the current movement analogous with that of 1776 results in a curious, mind-boggling juxtaposition of terms. In short, today's revolutionaries who wish to cloak themselves in the American flag and identify with the men of 1776 have missed the mark. A broad gulf continues to separate the Minutemen of the 1770s from the Weathermen of the 1970s. Those witnesses subpoenaed before the House investigating subcommittee in the summer of 1966 masqueraded in the costumes of Patriots while their ideas and rhetoric betrayed the real meaning of the American Revolution.

The Declaration's classic exposition of the principle of political equality offers a major clue to the relevance of 1776. Jefferson's assertion that all men are created equal and endowed with the same inalienable rights was to become America's "standard maxim." This ultimate goal of achieving a more equitable distribution of power and wealth without sacrificing our traditional liberties is the task to which America should address itself on the eve of the bicentennial anniversary. This does not mean that Americans have relinquished the right to revolution. Nor should they. Modern history has demonstrated that those nations that failed to recognize this right have been subject to violent tumults. But, in assessing the relevance of 1776 to contemporary America, primacy should be given to the "standard maxim" that the Founders proclaimed. Then the right of revolution, which they also heralded, can be viewed in its proper perspective.

Notes

1. U.S., Congress, House, Committee on Un-American Activities, *On Bills to Make Punishable Assistance to Enemies of the U.S. in Time of Undeclared War, Hearings,* before a subcommittee of the Un-American Activities Committee, on H.R. 12047, H.R. 14925, H.R. 16175, H.R. 17140, and H.R. 17194, 89th Cong., 2d sess., 1966, p. 965.

2. *The New York Times,* August 17, 1966, p. 24.

3. Arthur M. Schlesinger, "America's Influence: Our Ten Contributions to Civilization," *The Atlantic* (March 1959), 65.

4. Richard B. Morris, *The Emerging Nations and the American Revolution* (New York: Harper & Row, 1970), pp. 178–223.

5. This excerpt from President Kennedy's White House address of March 13, 1961, is cited in Arnold J. Toynbee's *America and the World Revolution* (New York: Oxford University Press, 1962), p. 218.

6. *The New York Times,* July 4, 1971, p. 26.

7. Leo Strauss and Joseph Cropsey, Eds., *A History of Political Philosophy,* 5th ed. (Chicago: Rand McNally, 1969), p. 462.

8. Carl L. Becker, *The Declaration of Independence: A Study in the History of Political Ideas* (New York: Vintage, 1942), pp. 14–15.

9. David Hawke, *A Transaction of Free Men: the Birth and Course of the Declaration of Independence* (New York: Scribner's, 1964), p. 149.

10. Staughton Lynd, *Intellectual Origins of American Radicalism* (New York: Vintage, 1969), p. 7.

11. *Ibid.,* p. 10.

12. At times Lynd has come dangerously close to doing so. See *Studies on the Left,* VI (January-February 1966), 49.

13. John R. Coyne, Jr., "The Kunstler Constituency," *National Review* (May 5, 1970), 467.

14. See especially *U.S. News & World Report* (April 27, 1970), 67–71; *The New Republic* (May 2, 1970), 9–10; and *Life* (May 1, 1970), 4.

15. William O. Douglas, *An Almanac of Liberty* (Garden City, New York: Doubleday, 1954), p. 3.

16. *Ibid., Points of Rebellion* (New York: Random House, 1970), p. 97.

17. Victor S. Navasky, "Right On With Lawyer William Kunstler," *The New York Times Magazine* (April 19, 1970), 88.

18. *Ibid.,* p. 92.

19. *The New York Times,* April 17, 1970, p. 44.

20. *Ibid.*

21. Abbie Hoffman, *Revolution for the Hell of It* (New York: Dial, 1968), p. 9.

22. Jerry Rubin, *Do It!: Scenarios of the Revolution* (New York: Ballantine, 1970), p. 37.

23. *U.C.L.A. Daily Bruin* (April 20, 1970), p. 1.

24. Rubin, *Do It!,* p. 39.

25. Eldridge Cleaver, *Soul On Ice* (New York: Dell, 1968), p. 134.

26. Rubin, *Do It!,* p. 123.

27. Tom Hayden, *Trial* (New York: Holt, Rinehart and Winston, 1970), p. 157.

28. Carl L. Becker, *The History of Political Parties in the Province of New York, 1760-1776* (Madison: University of Wisconsin Press, 1909), p. 5.

29. Jack P. Greene, "The Flight from Determinism: A Review of the Recent Literature on the Coming of the American Revolution, *South Atlantic Quarterly,* LXI (Spring 1962), 256-257.

30. See Jesse Lemisch's brilliant essay entitled "The American Revolution Seen from the Bottom Up" which appears in Barton J. Bernstein, Ed., *Towards A New Past: Dissenting Essays in American History* (New York: Vintage, 1969), pp. 3-45.

31. Merrill Jensen, "Democracy and the American Revolution," *Huntington Library Quarterly, XX* (August 1957), 321-341; Jackson Turner Main, "Results of the American Revolution," *The Historian,* **XXI** (August 1969), 539-554.

32. *Oxford English Dictionary,* 1933.

33. Staughton Lynd, *Class Conflict, Slavery, & the United States Constitution* (Indianapolis: Bobbs-Merrill, 1967), pp. 12-13.

34. Richard B. Morris, *The American Revolution Reconsidered* (New York: Harper & Row, 1968), pp. 83-84.

35. Kwame Nkrumah, *Consciencism: Philosophy and Ideology for Decolonization and Development with Particular Reference to the African Revolution* (New York: Monthly Review Press, 1964), p. 108.

36. *Black Panther,* December 6, 1969, cited by Philip S. Foner, Ed., *The Black Panthers Speak* (Philadelphia: Lippincott, 1970), p. 71.

37. Cleaver, *Soul On Ice,* pp. 112-113.

38. Foner, *The Black Panthers Speak,* pp. 2-4.

39. Hayden, *Trial,* pp. 150-168.

40. *Ibid.,* p. 160.

41. *Ibid.,* p. 162.
42. Hayden, *Trial,* pp. 150–152.
43. *OED.*
44. *Ibid.*

FROM TWO . . .

During the post-Revolutionary era (1783–1789) such problems as an unstable economy, diplomatic impotence, and the specter of political anarchy convinced nationalists like James Madison and James Wilson that a nation would have to be forged out of the 13 quarrelsome states of the confederation. The ensuing debate over the nature of this potentially large republic did not subside with the ratification of the Constitution in 1789 and has been carried into the 1970s. Today there are those who question the relevancy of this eighteenth-century document to the political, social, and economic complexities of twentieth-century America. From both the right and left of our political spectrum this question has been raised: "The Constitution: Has It Outlived Its Usefulness?"

. . . ON TO THREE

THREE

THE CONSTITUTION: HAS IT OUTLIVED ITS USEFULNESS?

FRED R. MABBUTT

During the Presidential elections of 1964 bumper stickers blanketing the electoral countryside announced the new trinity of holiness in America, "I believe in God, the Constitution, and Goldwater." About the sacredness of the first two entities there was little doubt in the American mind. The third, however, was more in question, as candidate Goldwater was left holding the charge on November 2 when the electoral dynamite exploded to give Lyndon Johnson his second term as president with the largest popular majority (61.1%) in modern American history.[1]

By contrast to the ephemeral shooting-star appearance of Barry Goldwater in the political heavens, the Constitution has been the veritable Rock of Ages for most Americans. Liberals and Conservatives may quarrel over such things as civil rights, foreign aid, and welfare, but historically they have first translated their differences into constitutional parlance and debated their disagreements as a legal issue.[2] Thus the two most powerful issues in America before the Civil War—slavery and national industrial development—were contested over the proper interpretation of the Constitution by such constitutional lawyers and theorists as Daniel Webster, John C. Calhoun, Thomas Hart Benton, and Abraham Lincoln. The more acrimonious the Liberal and Conservative arguments over the meaning of the Constitution became, the more entrenched was their homage to that document.

Even after the Civil War, with westward expansion and the new immigration, the Constitution was taken for granted by native and immigrant alike as the portal to the fulfillment of the Horatio Alger myth, or what William James called "the bitch-goddess Success." In spite of the fact that "Robber Barons" often used the Constitution for their own selfish purposes, proving Samuel Johnson's dictum about patriotism being the last refuge of scoundrels, the Captains of Industry managed to blend the capitalist legend with the Constitution so cleverly that both capitalism and the Constitution became symbols of sacrosanctity.

This fact of our political past is what makes our political present unique. Again Conservatives and Liberals confront each other ideologically. Again they stand in surprising agreement regarding their views of the Constitution: In the past they were filled with an inspired constitutional worship; today they are consumed with displeasure, and, as Martin Diamond has put it, "the more liberal or conservative the writer, the likelier and fuller the agreement."[3]

From the Right we see the late Senator Everett Dirksen's effort to rewrite the Constitution to restrict a part of the Bill of Rights and undo the reapportionment decisions of the 1960s nearing success. Of the 34 state legislatures needed to ask Congress to call a new Constitutional Convention 33 have already done so, and the American people may witness their first Constitutional Convention since the one held at Philadelphia in 1787.

Not to be denied, the Left has engaged in its own bit of constitutional rewriting. Most prominent among their proposals is the "model" constitution written by Rexford Tugwell and 150 experts at the Center for the Study of Democratic Institutions in Santa Barbara, California. Envisioning a clean break with the 1787 Constitution, Mr. Tugwell insists that he has "been as American as apple pie [in his new constitution] but made with the best apples and baked in an electric oven, not one attached to an old firewood stove." [4]

Although there is no doubt regarding the merit of Thomas Jefferson's famous maxim, that "The earth belongs to the living, not to the dead," [5] so momentous an occasion as rewriting the oldest written constitution in the world requires a sober examination of the proposals, Left and Right.

The Conservative·Call for a Second Constitutional Convention

The seeds of Conservative displeasure with the 1787 Constitution can be traced to June 26, 1962. On that day the Supreme Court handed down its school prayer decision in *Engle v. Vitale.*[6] By a 6 to 1 majority the Court struck down a 22-word prayer composed by the New York Board of Regents for use in the New York public schools. The reaction to the decision on the part of Conservatives was spontaneous and emotional. One Southern Senator, jelling his segregationist views with his anguish over the school prayer decision, lamented, "They [the Supreme Court] have taken God out of the schools and put the Nigras in." [7]

In that same year the Court handed down its first reapportionment decision in *Baker v. Carr,* followed in 1964 by *Wesberry v. Sanders* and *Reynolds v. Sims.*[8] In those decisions the Court enforced the "equal protection of the law" clause of the Fourteenth Amendment and ordered that the rural-conservative grip on legislative districts— state and federal—be broken.

State and federal legislative districts had been drawn to over-represent rural-conservative interests in flagrant violation of the equal rights of its citizens. Georgia, which was the state involved in *Wesberry v. Sanders,* had one district with as few as 272,154 citizens in it, whereas the largest contained 823,680, or three times the population of the smaller district.[9] In ordering that congressional reapportionment—and later that of both state legislative chambers—be drawn with an eye to equalizing population as closely as "practicable," a large number of rural-conservative legislators faced the loss of their districts and jobs as the districts were shifted to population centers in the cities and suburbs.

In 1965 and 1966 Senator Dirksen, a down-state conservative from Illinois, attempted to restore the power that was seeping away from men of his persuasion to the more liberal cities and suburbs of America by initiating a constitutional amendment that would permit the states to apportion at least one of its chambers on some basis other than population.

Thus by 1965 two constitutional amendments were being circulated by the Conservative forces of both political parties in America: the Dirksen amendment on reapportionment and the School Prayer Amendment to "put God back into the schools." Beyond this, Dirksen and the Conservatives had circulated among the 50 state legislatures a petition to call for a new Federal Constitutional Convention to provide them with greater discretion in their efforts to rewrite the Constitution. Rallying their forces, conservative units of the U.S. Chamber of Commerce, the Farm Bureau, and the National Association of Manufacturers waged an all-out campaign to exert pressure on state legislatures to call for a constitutional convention.[10]

By July 1967, 32 state legislatures had signed their petition, which meant that when two more states affixed their signatures "Congress . . . will be faced for the first time in history with implementing the provision in Article V of the Constitution specifying that it call such a convention upon application of two-thirds of the states." [11]

The year 1967 represented the high-water mark in the conservative effort to obtain a new constitutional convention. By the end of that year most of the states had reapportioned their legislatures, and with those bodies now in the hands of men who had been elected under the new system interest in the proposal waned but did not die. In its wake, however, a number of critically important questions remained unanswered; for example, how long does such a petition stay alive? What may be considered a valid state petition? Can states rescind their earlier approval (as Utah attempted to do in 1969)?[12] What would prevent a runaway convention from going far beyond the aim of its sponsors and indulging in a wholesale rewriting of the country's basic charter, including a revision of the Bill of Rights?

The latter concern is not an idle one. With the attack on religious freedom by Representative Chalmers Wylie (R-Ohio), the First Amendment's prohibition against the governmental "establishment of religion" may well be repealed. Falling only 28 votes shy of the necessary two-thirds approval by Congress in November 1971, his School Prayer Amendment would give to government still *another* control over American freedom by permitting the states to impose a religious ceremony on children in public schools. As University of Chicago Law Professor Philip B. Kurland has noted, "At best, the proposed amendment invites state-imposed religious dogma and religious strife; at worst, it assures them."[13]

In response to the "latter-day revival of Calhounian gospel" during the late 1960s and early 1970s,[14] a thirty-third state has added its approval to the Convention petition; moving the nation within one vote of calling its Second Constitutional Convention. Perhaps remembering that the delegates to the First Constitutional Convention of 1787 did not follow the written instructions given them by their state governments to *revise* the Articles of Confederation but rather that they *destroyed* it and replaced it with a new constitution, Senator Sam Ervin (D-North Carolina) contrived a Federal Constitutional Convention Procedures Bill to prohibit a convention from proposing or adopting any constitutional change that differed from the subject matter for which the state legislatures had requested the convention originally.

Congress has yet to enact it into law, although the Senate has endorsed the bill by acclamation.[15] Ironically, Senator Ervin's bill may *facilitate* rather than retard the calling of the convention. Although vaguely attempting to limit the scope of a constitutional convention if summoned, Ervin's bill, by setting forth guidelines for the submission of petitions, will make it much more difficult for Congress to challenge the nonself-executing language of Article V which says "Congress *shall* call a Convention . . ." on request of two-thirds of the states.[16]

The Liberal Call
For a New Constitution

By comparison the Left Wing of American politics has not been
nearly so ambitious in their efforts to bring about a Second Constitutional Convention. They have largely remained in their ivory
towers. As their "Refounding Father"—Rexford Tugwell—has admitted,[17] they may "never be able to present a convention, if there
should be one, with an agreed draft of a new Constitution; but it
[the Tugwell Constitution] might approximate the Virginia Resolves"[18] which had been the basis of the earlier 1787 Constitution.[19]

Acknowledging that his "model" constitution represents a "radical"
break with the past, Tugwell envisions the disappearance of the 50
states in favor of roughly 20 republics, each with about 10 million
people or "no less than five per cent of the whole people."[20] His
hope is to eliminate geographical "distortions" that obstruct action
for the common good.

Reflecting his personal experiences during the Depression when
many of his New Deal farm policies were thwarted by the Supreme
Court, Tugwell calls for a strengthening of the presidency and a
weakening of the judiciary. Compliant with this, Tugwell's charter
would establish one presidential term that would last nine years and
would fragment the judiciary into nine levels over which a "principal
justice" would preside for a period of 12 years rather than for life.

One of those levels, a separate High Court of the Constitution,
would advise the House of Representatives on the constitutionality
of its legislation when requested to do so by the Senate. Although
the House would initiate all legislation, the consent of the Senate
would be required for it to become law and it could override the
High Court's "advisory opinions."

Tugwell's legislature would little resemble today's. The House of
Representatives would consist of 400 members elected for three-year
terms, 100 of them at large. All committee chairmen would be
appointed annually by the Speaker of the House and would be
required to come exclusively from the at-large membership. No
chairman would be permitted to serve for more than six years.

Insulating the Senate from control by the public, its members
would serve for life. All former presidents, vice-presidents, governors
general of their republics with more than seven years service, and

unsuccessful candidates for the presidency and vice presidency who gained at least 30 percent of the vote would be entitled to a Senate seat. A dozen others would be appointed by the President, the Principal Justice could appoint five, and the House, three from its own membership.

The popular branch of government—the House of Representatives—would be hemmed in on all sides by the Senate, the High Court, and the President. Not only could the High Court guide their legislative efforts with "advisory opinions" requested by the Senate but the Senate could veto any House-passed legislation by a majority vote. Although the House could override the Senate veto with a two-thirds majority, the President could also veto House action and could not be overruled without a three-fourths approval by the House.

The Tugwell "model" also calls for three additional branches of government—the Electoral, the Planning, and the Regulatory. These branches, headed by an "overseer," would plan and police elections, design American six and twelve-year economic plans, and supervise the national economy.

There would be no Bill of Rights, although many of the freedoms guaranteed by that document are scattered throughout his constitution. On the whole, however, the liberal Tugwell constitution views individual rights as potentially in conflict with the "national interests and general welfare" and the cause of "near paralysis." [21]

Like many Conservatives, Tugwell believes that the present Constitution has outlived its usefulness and that a new one is in order. Although the Conservatives have moved the state legislatures within one vote of calling for a Second Constitutional Convention, the Liberals have been busy rewriting the Constitution in order that their model—like the Virginia Resolves—might become the basis of America's second constitution.

Conclusion

It would seem that both the Liberals and the Conservatives subscribe to the theory that argues that political life is created not so much by social structure, culture, or history but by constitutionalism, that is, the differences in the rules by which a people abide.

There are a number of obvious peculiarities in this theory. Some countries like the United Kingdom have no single codified document that can be called a constitution. Also constitutions do not necessarily determine a nation's political behavior at all, as demonstrated by Stalin's Constitution of 1936 which professed adherence to democratic values but practiced something quite different.

A nation's constitution is never found in the document itself but rather in the minds and attitudes of the people to whom the rules apply. Nations like France have been slow in learning this lesson. When the French are unhappy with their political life, they simply write a new constitution. Because of this France has had 18 constitutions since 1791—compared with one for the United States—and no regime lasted more than 15 years until the establishment of the Third Republic in 1871. Cruelly manifesting this tragedy of French constitutional life is a French advertisement that proclaims, "The Republics pass, X's paint remains." [22]

Rarely, if ever, does a constitution survive a second draft. This would be like Moses descending Mt. Sinai with the sacred writ and, no sooner having presented it to the chosen people, suggesting to them amendments or even the abandonment of the Ten Commandments in favor of a better set of rules.

A people can have only one beginning. The sacredness of a constitution that invites obedience—which Goldwater hoped to transfer to his presidential ambitions in 1964—cannot reoccur in a second or third constitutional beginning.

Historically, neither the Liberals nor the Conservatives have been totally happy with the Constitution. What one has deplored, the other has applauded. As Professor Diamond has pointed out, this fundamental difference between the Liberal and Conservative view of the Constitution which paradoxically brings them together in their antipathy toward that document can be understood best in terms of Madison's famous statement in *Federalist* 51. [23]

> In framing a government which is to be administered by men over men, the great difficulty lies in this: you must first enable the government to control the governed; and in the next place oblige it to control itself. A *dependence on the people* is, no doubt, the primary control on the government; but experience has taught mankind the necessity of *auxiliary precautions*.

Two elements can be seen in the Madisonian plan: "dependence on the people," which is much preferred by Liberals, and "auxiliary precautions" like federalism, separation of powers, checks and balances, and judicial review, which are much more fancied by Conservatives. Thus Liberals and Conservatives alike *separate* the two elements that form a consistent *whole* in the original Constitution.

Although Tugwell unabashedly obliterates parochial or geographical interests in favor of the *general* welfare, the Conservatives fight rear-guard actions to preserve or impose *local* control over such issues as school prayer, busing of children to public schools, and reapportionment.

The Founding Fathers attempted to blend these two interests by combining *territorial* democracy with *majoritarian* democracy. They did not want to fall into that Marxian cul-de-sac by solely concerning themselves with the quantity in our democracy nor did they want to thwart the prudential will of the majority. No one has more eloquently stated this principle of the Constitution of 1787 than Thomas Jefferson in his First Inaugural Address:

> All, too, will bear in mind this sacred principle, that though the will of the majority is in all cases to prevail, that will to be rightful must be reasonable; that the minority possess their equal rights, which equal law must protect, and to violate would be oppression.

The Founders solidly embraced the principle of majority rule in the Constitution of 1787, albeit with checks on that majority to prevent it from tyrannizing the minority. Although Woodrow Wilson correctly insisted in 1917 that "The World Must Be Made Safe for Democracy," the Founders in 1787 correctly understood that "Democracy Must Be Made Safe for the World."

They understood that majorities, as well as minorities, could be rather vicious at times. It does not take a professional student of history to recall that Socrates was killed by an Athenian democracy or that Hitler's rise to power in the Weimar Republic of Germany had something to do with democracy. Indeed, the schema of Marx and Engels had a great deal to do with majority rule, even though solely a numerical and proletarianized majority, which established its dictatorship by domestic and international convulsion.

The problem, as the Founders saw it, was to create a polity consistent with the principles generated by the American Revolution. This meant that they had to create a regime that would produce prudential leadership, one that would tyrannize neither the majority nor minority and still maintain decent representation.

There is no doubt that the Founders assessed democracy realistically, unabashedly identifying its defects. Yet it is important to note that they *accepted* it in principle, merely insisting that one should not whistle in the dark in regard to those deficiencies. Taking what they called "auxillary precautions," the Founders emphasized throughout the *Federalist Papers* that the inconveniences of democratic government could be remedied only by democratic devices.

Their theoretical invention of federalism represents but one of the mechanisms devised by the Founders to create the kind of majority we want, namely, a majority fragmented or deflected from its "schemes of oppression." By fragmenting the majority according to the federal principle, thus creating *a* majority of shifting coalitions and dividing society into majority and minority factions vertically rather than horizontally, the Founders largely succeeded in creating a majority-minority schism that did not follow the strata of class, section, or religious differentiation. Instead, it cut deeply through those strata and left on either side of the cleavage a similar cross section of the nation. Thus the numerical majority ruled, but it was not *the* majority but rather *a* majority, nationally distributed.

It was correctly not the desire of the Founders, nor the *telos* of this polity, merely to create a democratic regime. Their task was to create a particular kind of democratic regime. Nations, like people, do not have to strive simply to be a nation or a person. The real task is to assume the best form rather than the worst. That the Founders took "auxilliary precautions" while maintaining a "dependence on the people" to ensure that we would have the former kind of democracy has in no small measure contributed to the legitimacy and sacrosanctity of our present Constitution and to the success of this, the now oldest, democratic republic in the world.

Both the Liberal and the Conservative demands for a new constitutional convention represent an effort to implement one, but not both, of the elements of the "Madisonian" constitution which sought to make democracy safe for the world. If either succeeded, America might well end up with minority rule or rule by an unbridled majority which could run roughshod over the rights of the minority.

We should not be unwilling to change the Constitution to meet the changing exigencies of American life. We should be sure, how-ever—to use Mr. Madison's famous phrase in *Federalist* 10—that the cure is not worse than the disease.

After viewing Tugwell's "model" constitution, which lacks a Bill of Rights but has a Senate for life, a House pinched-in from all sides, and an overseer of nationalized elections, we are led to wonder if his cure for "governmental stalemate" is worse than the disease. Equally, after examining the Conservative efforts to restrict the First Amendment's 200-year-old requirement that the state not meddle in church affairs and their efforts to base legislative representation on trees and rocks rather than people, we are also tempted to wonder whether Bismarck was correct when he said, "God looks out for fools, drunks, and the United States of America." We would be wrong. A better answer would be that the safeguards implanted in the Constitution of 1787 by our Founders provided for such exigencies.

Notes

1. Congressional Quarterly, *Politics in America* (Washington, D.C.: Congres-sional Quarterly Service, 1969), p. 126.

2. Max Lerner, "Constitution and Court As Symbols," *Yale Law Journal*, 46 (June 1937), 1301.

3. Martin Diamond, "Conservatives, Liberals, and the Constitution," *Left, Right and Center* (Chicago: Rand McNally Public Affairs Series, 1967), p. 60.

4. "Founding Fathers Wouldn't Know the Constitution, Tugwell Version," *The National Observer*, September 14, 1970, p. 7.

5. J. P. Folly, Ed., *The Jefferson Cyclopedia*, Vo. I (1900, 1967), p. 199.

6. *Engle v. Vitale*, 370 U.S. 421 (1962).

7. H. Frank Hay, Jr., *Liberty in the Balance* (New York: McGraw-Hill, 1964), p. 78.

8. *Baker v. Carr*, 369 U.S. 186 (1962); *Wesberry v. Sanders*, 376 U.S. 1 (1964); *Reynolds v. Sims*, 377 U.S. 533 (1964)

9. "The Supreme Court Draws the Line," *Newsweek* (March 2, 1964), 15–17; *Wesberry v. Sanders*, 376 U.S. 1 (1964).

10. Congressional Quarterly, *Representation and Apportionment* (Washington, D.C.: Congressional Quarterly Service, 1966), pp. 33–34.

11. Theodore C. Sorensen, "The Quiet Campaign To Rewrite The Constitution," *Saturday Review* (July 15, 1967), 17.

12. Kenneth Reich, "1-Man, 1-Vote Challenge Jeopardized," *Los Angeles Times,* August 25, 1969.

13. Philip B. Kurland, "On School Prayer—a Threat to Religion," *Los Angeles Times,* October 31, 1971. The House defeated the Wylie amendment with 240 giving approval to 162 who voted against it.

14. James J. Kilpatrick, "Constitutional Craftsman on the Defensive," *Los Angeles Times,* November 2, 1971.

15. The Senate approved the bill on October 20, 1971, by a margin of 84–0.

16. Article V. Emphasis added. Because there is no precedent here, it is not known whether Congress *must* call a convention on request.

17. The Center For The Study Of Democratic Institutions at Santa Barbara refers to Tugwell in *The Center Magazine* as a "Refounding Father." See *The Center Magazine,* **I,** No. 3 (March 1968), 1.

18. *Ibid.*

19. Martin Diamond, "What The Farmers Meant By Federalism," found in Robert A. Goldwin (Ed.), *A Nation of States* (Chicago: Rand McNally, 1966), pp. 24–41.

20. Rexford G. Tugwell, "Introduction to a Constitution for a United Republics of America. Version XXXVII," *The Center Magazine,* **III,** No. 5 (September 1970), 25. A complete copy of Tugwell's constitution may be found in this edition.

21. Tugwell, "Introduction to a Constitution," p. 17.

22. D. W. Brogan quoted in Fred R. Mabbutt, "Italy and the Fourth French Republic: A Study in Political Stability," *CCSSQ* (Summer, 1971), 16.

23. Diamond, "Conservatives, Liberals, and the Constitution," p. 61. Emphasis added to *Federalist* 51.

FROM THREE . . .

During the 1790s the Founders attempted to implement the
Constitution by inaugurating the Hamiltonian economic system.
Just after the banking, tariff, and debt-funding measures were
passed into law, however, the entire program was jeopardized
by the revival in 1793 of hostilities between Great Britain and
France. To protect the newly established republic from the
dangers of war and foreign influence President George Washington proclaimed the advantages of pursuing a policy of neutrality and political noninvolvement in the affairs of Europe,
thereby laying the foundations for America's traditional isolationism. Always central to our foreign policy, its efficacy was
challenged during the post-World War II period, but recent
trends indicate a re-emergence of interest in its basic tenets.

. . . ON TO FOUR

If America winds up the war in Vietnam in failure and an image is developed that the war was fought only by stupid scoundrels, there would be a wave of isolationism . . . , which would embrace the U.S. role everywhere.

President Richard M. Nixon
The New York Times, March 10, 1971

FOUR

THE "NEW ISOLATIONISM": RHETORIC OR REALITY?

THOMAS J. OSBORNE

Today America is undergoing the most searching examination of its foreign policy foundations since the birth of the Republic. The recent burial of democracy in South Korea, coupled with the Vietnam debacle and its unfortunate domestic consequences, has caused many Americans to doubt the efficacy of globalism and containment. A younger postwar generation, largely unfamiliar with the menacing encroachments of Stalinist Russia in the late 1940s, is inclined to reject the basic postulates of American diplomacy during the last 25 years. Amid the confusion of the present some are looking to the past for sensible guidelines on which to chart the future course of our foreign policy. In view of the current difficulties and setbacks arising out of foreign embroilments, it is not surprising that concerned citizens, as well as political leaders and trained publicists, should turn to the counsel of our Founding Fathers.

If Americans have ever had a Delphic Oracle to consult when their nation reached a diplomatic crossroad, it has been Washington's Farewell Address of September 17, 1796. In the 1790s, just as in the 1970s, foreign policy issues tended to overshadow and shape the course of domestic politics. Before turning over the reins of power in the midst of a deepening Franco-American crisis, President Washington cautioned America's new leaders "to steer clear of permanent alliances with any portion of the foreign world." [1] As far as the immediate future was concerned, Washington sagely advised:

> The great rule of conduct for us in regard to foreign nations,
> is, in extending our commercial relations, to have with them
> as little political connection as possible. [2]

Neutrality in times of war and political noninvolvement in time of peace: these were the lineaments of America's traditional isolationist policy. To the scant three and a half million inhabitants of an infant nation, who were separated from the vicissitudes of European politics by 3000 miles of ocean that took six weeks in the crossing, this advice seemed eminently sound.

A number of factors coalesced during the nineteenth century to shore up America's isolationist posture. Washington's pronouncements were given fresh restatement by President James Monroe in his celebrated speech of December 2, 1823. Observing that the Atlantic ocean divided the world into two spheres, Monroe stated that the New World had to insulate itself from the intrigues and advances of the Old. Henceforth European colonization in the Western Hemisphere would be regarded as an "unfriendly act." Thus the noninvolvement principle was given vigorous reiteration. A word of qualification is in order, however. President Monroe, like Washington earlier, did not subscribe to a dogmatic, simon-pure form of isolationism. As Dexter Perkins points out, Monroe was not averse to entering a temporary military alliance with England to ward off an impending invasion of South America by the Holy Alliance powers. [3] At any rate, Monroe's classic exposition of the isolationist creed has been the object of profound, if at times misguided, veneration.

The *Pax Britannica* which followed the Napoleonic Wars released American manpower and resources for westward expansion across the North American continent. This vast migration toward the Pacific aggravated the internal problems of sectionalism and slavery, thereby polarizing Americans for more than half a century. In addition, the completion of a transcontinental railroad network, urbanization, industrialization, and severe economic depressions during the 1870s and 1890s contributed to America's preoccupation with domestic affairs during the latter half of the nineteenth century. Not until after the Spanish-American War of 1898 was the American ship of state jarred loose from its isolationist moorings and set adrift in the troubled waters of European politics and overseas wars.

America's failure to join the League of Nations at the end of World War I signaled the return to isolationism. Liberals disillusioned by Wilson's "sellout" at Versailles lent their angry voices to the swelling chorus of protest against the "League of Robber Nations." [4] Although the United States rejected collective security and did not enter the World Court in 1926, as an unscathed and unrivaled creditor nation it assumed some obligation to dispense relief in Europe and to supervise the payment of reparations. It should be noted, however, that even these limited measures of involvement were in part occasioned by our high tariff policy which severely curtained European trade with the United States. In essence, during the 1920s the United States pursued simultaneously a foreign policy of political isolationism and economic internationalism. In this way we maintained our political freedom of action so that we could advance our economic power globally without being tied to any bloc of nations. The following decade did not allow us the luxury of enjoying both freedom of political action and a burgeoning foreign commerce.

America's isolationist outlook hardened during the depression-ridden 1930s. The repudiation of European war debts owed to the United States probably bred many isolationists. Also the wave of military aggression in Europe, Asia, and Africa played a major role in whipping up isolationist sentiment on Capital Hill and throughout the country. While Germany was reacquiring the Saar and denouncing the disarmament clauses pertaining to her in the Versailles Treaty, Senator Gerald P. Nye's investigating committee released a 1400-page bombshell in 1935–1936 which indicted an international cartel of bankers and munitions makers for pressuring America into war in 1917. Shocked and frightened by the Nye Committee report (and unable to ferret out its numerous non sequiturs), the public insisted that Congress take steps to prevent such a baneful recurrence in the tinderbox atmosphere of the mid-1930s.

As war clouds gathered over Ethiopia, Congress passed into law the first of a series of neutrality measures gauged to keep America out of an imminent European conflagration. Selig Adler, a leading historian of American isolationism, regards these acts as "the supreme triumph of the isolationist concept." The hopes of America Firsters and the other champions of the "Fortress America" concept, i.e., that a properly defended Western Hemisphere would be impregnable, evaporated with the rain of Japanese bombs that fell from the skies over Oahu on that fateful December morning in 1941.

It took the holocaust of world war to swing the foreign policy pendulum from isolationism to collective security. Under the latter policy it is presupposed that an attack on any one of a concert of avowedly peace-seeking nations would be regarded as an attack on all. In the event of such aggression, the member states would intervene collectively and impose sanctions or exercise military force to restore the status quo. Obviously the tenets of collective security were antithetical to those of isolationism. One could not remain neutral if a party to the regional alliance were attacked, and membership in such a treaty organization would necessarily result in fettered peacetime involvements of a political nature.

After witnessing the horrors of genocide and atomic warfare America and her leaders became convinced that more than ever before the stakes of all-out war were appallingly high. Our refusal to join the League of Nations and the League's inability to prevent the outbreak of World War II convinced many Americans that the responsibility for maintaining world peace would necessarily devolve on a formidable body of dedicated nations joined together in a formal manner by written commitments. Doubtless it was this realization, coupled with the haunting memory of the blatantly partisan Versailles Treaty debate, that led to the Senate's overwhelming approval of America's entry into the United Nations in August 1945.

Russian obstructionism on the Security Council and her expansion into the newly created power vacuums in Eastern Europe and Asia ended America's brief honeymoon with collective security, but the marriage was far from dissolved. Although remaining active in the United Nations, American policy makers decided that a back-up system of military alliances was needed to check Red encroachments in Europe and elsewhere. The upshot was the negotiation of a network of regional collective security pacts that committed America to the defense of 44 nations scattered across the face of the globe. The containment of Soviet advances was the desired end while regional security alliances, such as NATO and SEATO, coupled with Marshall Plan aid provided the means. Significantly, U.S. membership in NATO (1949) constituted America's first long-term military commitment since the Franco-American alliance of 1778, which took the neutrality-minded Founders 22 years to abrogate.

Because the containment doctrine by nature is antithetical to the nonalliance principle of isolationism, the former will serve as a useful foil against which we can contrast the "isolationist" developments of the late 1960s and early 1970s. For this reason it is necessary to recall briefly the basic postulates of the mature containment theory. It should be noted that the full-blown thesis goes far beyond the rather modest, if ambiguous, proposals outlined by George F. Kennan in his *Foreign Affairs* article of July 1947.

In its latest form the theory of containment embraces at least four key assumptions, nearly all of which have been subject to mounting criticism in recent years.[5] First, conflicting ideological systems, such as capitalism and communism, will probably lead to a military clash between the respective nations that espouse these systems. Second, communism is a monolithic movement controlled by the Kremlin, whence its sinister plans are conceived for the overthrow of all noncommunist regimes. Third, Russian advances across America's proclaimed defense perimeter, for whatever reason, constitute a prima facie threat to parliamentary democracy and therefore to American security. This threat was especially ominous because it was believed that the fall of one country to communist rule, that is, Moscow domination, would inevitably have a domino effect on that country's neighbors. Fourth, Soviet expansionist tendencies must, if necessary, be checked by superior American military force.

Having scanned the broad historical and conceptual background of American isolationism and its antithesis, collective security, we can now step into the foreground of the present and look for signs of an isolationist renaissance. First we shall gauge the public sentiment with respect to isolationism and then determine to what extent, if any, this sentiment has been translated into foreign policy.

While acknowledging the growing impatience with the war in Southeast Asia, President Richard M. Nixon admitted that if a Gallup poll were taken at any time during his first administration it would have shown that the great majority of people "want to pull out of Vietnam . . . , pull three or more divisions out of Europe and . . . cut our defense budget."[6] The President's intuitive assessment of the general will received statistical support in a study by Albert Cantril and Charles Roll entitled *Hopes and Fears of the American People* (1971). These two public opinion experts reported that 77 percent of the American people agreed with the statement:

> We shouldn't think so much in international terms but concentrate more on our own national problems and building up our strength and prosperity at home.[7]

This figure represents a 22 percent increase since 1964, when the public's response to the same question was sampled by the Institute for International Social Research.

The inference to be drawn is not that Americans wish to withdraw from all political, military, and economic ties with the rest of the world. We have never done so and it seems ludicrous to suppose that we ever would. A more reasonable inference would be that the public has grown increasingly weary of nearly 10 years of expensive, unpopular, and indecisive containment warfare in Southeast Asia and that in their opinion the national interest would be served better by substantially reducing our overseas defense commitments. This view roughly comports with our isolationist tradition of remaining free from entangling permanent alliances so that republican institutions can be fostered at home.

It seems safe to say that few Americans feel that their nation is any more secure from attack as a result of our attempt to hold the Viet Cong at bay north of the 17th parallel. The low return on our Vietnam investment has raised fundamental questions about the efficacy of America's paramount role in NATO and other treaty organizations. Is our nation's core security any greater in the new age of sophisticated and proliferated thermonuclear weaponry as a result of these military alliances? Many Americans are no longer taking the affirmative answer for granted.

In addition to the Vietnam War, there are other important factors that have triggered the current isolationist reaction, not the least of which is that it is widely recognized that we now live in a dramatically different world from the one of a generation ago. The postwar division of the globe into bipolar spheres dominated by the United States and the Soviet Union has given way to a multipolar international environment composed of powerful, assertive newcomers like Japan, the People's Republic of China, and West Germany. President Nixon's unprecedented visits to Peking and Moscow in mid-1972 indicate that the ideological schism is no longer an insurmountable barrier to amicable relations between East and West. Also, America's once undisputed military and technological superiority over Russia was no longer confidently assumed after the launching of Sputnik in 1957. One by one, as numerous publicists as well as the President himself have pointed out, the old Cold War shibboleths have broken down[8] in a climate that is much more conducive to a reduced international role for the United States.

Finally, public support for interventionism has waned because of the growing skepticism about America's capacity to perform good works on an international scale. Connected with this is the increasing public concern with the domestic problems of racism, welfare, crime, pollution, and inflation. A poll conducted by Lou Harris and Associates in 1970 showed that 76 percent of the nation's college students believed that basic changes are needed in the American political and social system.[9] "What America cannot as yet do for itself," observes Johns Hopkins professor Robert W. Tucker, "it surely cannot do for others."[10]

Although there seems little reason to doubt the pervasiveness of isolationist sentiment, it is by no means clear that this popular outlook has materially altered the course of our diplomacy. There are indications, however, that the foreign policy pendulum is slowly swinging back in a neoisolationist direction, that is, toward a retreat from rather than an abandonment of our military commitments.

In his Guam address of 1969, as well as in several other foreign policy speeches, the President elaborated on the Nixon Doctrine which, in essence, proclaims that America will maintain a lower profile in international affairs. While disavowing any "intention of withdrawing from the world" in a major address before Congress on February 18, 1970, Nixon called for "more responsible participation by our foreign friends in their own defense." The President went on to renounce our global containment strategies of the past:

> America cannot—and will not—conceive all the plans, design all the programs, execute all the decisions, and undertake all the defense of the free nations of the world.[11]

The "low profile" announced in the Nixon Doctrine will permit a reduction in U.S. general-purpose troops stationed overseas and will help to put a ceiling on defense spending.[12] Our present operating assumption is that America's military security requires the capacity to prosecute simultaneously two major wars plus one smaller war elsewhere. Force reductions will enable the United States to fight a major war in Europe or in Asia, plus the contingency of one police action somewhere else. In theory, then, America's new defense projections will be based on our ability to wage one and a half rather than two and a half wars. In sum, one might hesitate to call these fundamental theoretical shifts "neoisolationist"; nevertheless, they do suggest that new parameters will be carefully designed to reduce the risk of unnecessary and costly unilateral meddling.

Theory aside, there are a number of indications that the United States is disengaging from political and military involvement in Asia and Europe. Although the Japanese-American security treaty no doubt will remain in effect for some time, Japanese-American relations have been altered because of Japan's growing defense capabilities and a hoped-for Sino-American *detente*. Nippon now has the eighth largest defense budget in the world and its government has earmarked $16 billion for military expenditures for the five-year period from 1972 to 1976. That country could probably become nuclear operational in a year or two. Acknowledging this expanding economic and military strength, the United States has returned Okinawa and is presently reducing the number of American bases in Japan. With respect to our commitments in Southeast Asia, Andrew J. Pierre, Hedley Bull, and other noted foreign-policy experts have predicted that after the withdrawal of American forces from Vietnam

"SEATO may come to have little meaning for the United States." [13]

Regarding our NATO obligations, it seems only a matter of time before a substantial reduction of America's 300,000 troops will take place. Two luminaries of the Senate Foreign Relations Committee, Chairman J. William Fulbright and Senator Mike Mansfield, worked to reduce by one-half the contingent of U.S. troops in NATO countries. American balance of payments deficits, coupled with the augmentation of the European Economic Community and France's nuclear deterrent power, have paved the way for a devolution of America's security responsibilities in Europe.

In view of the current diffusion of military power throughout the world, the virtual abandonment of our anticommunist foreign policy outlook, the reluctance of Americans to "democratize" the rest of the world, the general retrenchment of American military commitments, and our present nuclear capabilities, a plausible case can be made for a new isolationism. Professor Robert W. Tucker argues with compelling logic that America's massive and sophisticated nuclear arsenal (assuming parity with the Russians) gives this country as much of a protective shield as it will ever have or ever need if we are thinking in terms of sheer physical security.[14] If it is contended that this assumption is weakened by the lack of sure-proof surveillance techniques, the retort is that the same problem exists when the leading powers rely on conventional weaponry. So this objection does not stand. Were the Soviet Union to overrun all of Western Europe tomorrow, observes Tucker,

> that fact [would] not in any way establish a base for concluding that a thereby strengthened Soviet Union would be in a position to attack America without facing disastrous consequences.[15]

Clearly, no possible combination of conventional multilateral alliances could pose such an ominous threat of retaliation, for so little financial cost, as our storehouse of nuclear weaponry.

Some may argue that an isolationist policy would be impractical because American commerce would decline, thereby endangering our domestic economy. Although the American economy would suffer from a decline in trade, our principal commercial partners would suffer far more, asserts Tucker:

> In 1968, exports comprised 4 per cent of the GNP of the United
> States, but 10 per cent of the GNP of Japan, 14 per cent of
> the GNP of the United Kingdom, and 12 per cent of the GNP
> of Germany.[16]

What reason is there to think that nations dependent on trade with
the United States would choke off this commerce as a result of the
abrogation of our military alliances? The only reason to assume that
commercial and investment opportunities in the United States would
decline in the event of military withdrawal is to suppose that our
trading partners in Western Europe had been conquered by Russia
and that Japan had become an appendage of China. In view of the
rapidly growing defense capabilities of Western Europe and Japan,
the prospect of outside domination becomes increasingly remote.

A new isolationism would differ markedly from the "head in the
sand" policy of the interwar years, which, in addition to ignoring
real security dangers, was based on conspiracy theories, chauvinism,
and xenophobia. Instead, a prospective isolationist policy for America
would be predicated on awesome defense capabilities and a reduced
sense of chiliastic nationalism and certainly would not discourage
international cooperation for the resolution of worldwide problems.
It must be kept in mind that America's isolationist tradition does
not rule out all political relationships—only those that lead inexorably
to entangling military alliances.

It has been shown that isolationism is deeply ingrained in the
American experience. The advice of our Founding Fathers regarding
entangling alliances coincided propitiously in the nineteenth century
with Europe's distresses and the dynamic course of our internal
development. America's belated entry into World War I and our
subsequent refusal to join the League of Nations indicate that the
nation was extremely reluctant to think in terms of overseas political
and military responsibilities. During the interwar years of the twentieth century this salutary tradition hardened into an ugly dogma
that gripped the nation until the logic of events forced its repudiation
in December 1941. World War II and its tense aftermath inaugurated
a new era of collective security and global involvement during which
Cold Warriors persistently identified isolationism with provincialism
and appeasement.

Now, after a generation of containment warfare, the Munich appeasement syndrome has been superceded by the Vietnam futility lesson. Once again the logic of events seems conducive to an isolationist renaissance. That public opinion is favorable to the new drift toward isolationism seems apparent, but it is unlikely at this time that our foreign policy makers are prepared to withdraw from our alliances. Disengagement is a welcomed step in that direction but it is still too early to project how far the foreign affairs pendulum will swing beyond the "low profile" mark. As far as national policy is concerned, much of the discussion about isolationism remains rhetoric.

Notes

1. Henry Steele Commager, Ed., *Documents of American History* (8th ed., New York: Appleton-Century-Crofts, 1968), p. 174. It is important to note that at the time of his Farewell Address Washington was trying to abrogate the 1778 military alliance with France. Failure to do so, conceivably, could have resulted in one of two undesirable consequences. Either the United States could have been unwillingly drawn into the war on the side of France, or, in refusing to declare war on England, it could have been charged that our government did not honor its diplomatic commitments.

2. *Ibid.*

3. Dexter Perkins, *A History of the Monroe Doctrine* (Boston: Little, Brown, 1963), pp. 48–49.

4. Selig Adler, *The Isolationist Impulse: Its Twentieth Century Reaction* (New York: Free Press, 1957), p. 64.

5. Neal D. Houghton, Ed., *Struggle Against History: U.S. Foreign Policy in an Age of Revolution* (New York: Simon and Schuster, 1968), pp. 20–40. The chapter by Fred Warner Neal gives a solid exposition and critique of the postwar containment policy. For an excellent account of the New Left's opposition to containment warfare in Southeast Asia see Walter LaFeber's *America, Russia, and the Cold War, 1945–1971* (New York: Wiley, 1972), pp. 269–301.

6. Robert W. Tucker, *A New Isolationism: Threat or Promise?* (New York: Universe, 1972), p. 16.

7. Albert H. Cantril and Charles W. Roll, *Hopes and Fears of the American People* (New York: Universe, 1971), p. 42.

8. Richard M. Nixon, *U.S. Foreign Policy for the 1970's: A New Strategy for Peace* (Washington, D.C.: Government Printing Office, 1970), pp. 2–13.

9. James A. Johnson, "The New Generation of Isolationists," *Foreign Affairs* (October 1970), p. 139.

10. Tucker, *A New Isolationism*, p. 34.

11. Nixon, *U.S. Foreign Policy for the 1970's*, p. 6.

12. Andrew J. Pierre, "The Future of America's Commitments and Alliances," *Orbis* (Fall, 1972), 696.

13. *Ibid.*, p. 707.

14. Tucker, *A New Isolationism*, pp. 49–50.

15. *Ibid.*, p. 49.

16. Tucker, *A New Isolationism*, p. 61.

FROM FOUR . . .

America's isolationist policy has been pursued for a number of reasons, perhaps the most important of which has been to preserve republican institutions at home. Excessive foreign involvement has invariably bred factionalism and repression at home, as it did during the Quasi-War with France (1798–1800).

Our "splendid isolation" after the Napoleanic Wars permitted westward expansion across the North American continent. A major consequence of this movement was the heightening of sectional conflict between North and South over slavery, as new territories applied for admission to statehood. Hoping to steer Americans back to the principles of equality and liberty contained in the Declaration of Independence, Abraham Lincoln reminded the nation in 1858: "A house divided against itself cannot stand" and that "this government cannot endure permanently half-slave and half-free." In the 1970s America once again appears to be a house divided and, as in the past, race has exacerbated the conflict.

. . . ON TO FIVE

. . . all men are created equal . . .

Declaration of Independence

. . . nor [may any State] deny to any person within its jurisdiction the equal protection of the laws.

Fourteenth Amendment

FIVE

FROM
PLANTATION TO GHETTO:
EQUALITY IN AMERICA

FRED R. MABBUTT

Today, as America approaches the bicentennial commemoration of its *Declaration of Independence* in 1776, it does so in a more disordered condition than at any time in its history since the Great Depression of the 1930s or possibly the Civil War of more than 100 years ago. From California Governor Ronald Reagan's strident statement, "If it's to be a bloodbath, let it be now" to H. Rap Brown's declaration that violence is "as American as cherry pie," both black and white Americans have girded themselves to join battle in the wake of the urban riots of 1965 through 1967.

Three of these riots amounted to major civil convulsions. The 1965 Watts riot in Los Angeles resulted in 34 dead with more than 1000 injured in the violence, burning, and looting that encompassed more than 50 miles of the inner city. The 1967 Newark disturbance caused 23 deaths and required more than 4000 policemen and National Guardsmen to restore order. The bloodiest of the riots, however, occurred in 1967 in Detroit and left 43 dead and more than 1000 injured in the charred ruins of a city strangling in smoke.

Many have regarded these events, like the Civil War that preceded them, to be symptomatic of the breakdown of America's democratic process and evidence of the nation's betrayal of its basic philosophy, expressed in the *Declaration of Independence,* that "all men are created equal." We are told by some advocates of civil rights that our present dilemma hinges on the racism and/or hypocrisy of the Founding Fathers; that the *Declaration of Independence* is a fraud, which only "by remaining vague . . . could say all men were created equal"; that "inalienable rights never meant Negroes"; and that "nothing was more secure in the new Constitution of the United States than Negro slavery." [1]

This opinion is not new. Indeed, one may recall Lincoln's exculpatory letter of April 6, 1859, wherein he dealt with a similar assault on the principles of Jefferson by the proponents of slavery. In that letter Lincoln wrote:

> The principles of Jefferson are the definitions and axioms of free society. And yet they are denied and evaded, with no small show of success. One dashingly calls them "glittering generalities"; another bluntly calls them "self-evident lies"; . . . [2]

Ironically, this view of the *Declaration of Independence* and our present racial dilemma is one shared by advocates and adversaries of civil rights. As in Lincoln's day, it has had "no small show of success" and for that reason deserves consideration.

The American Cosmogony

Following the urban riots of the 1960s, President Lyndon Johnson appointed Governor Otto Kerner of Illinois to determine what happened, why it happened, and what could be done to prevent a recurrence. In the *Report of the National Advisory Commission* the 11-member Commission called on history to explain the crisis between black and white. Turning to the *Declaration of Independence*, they wrote that the statement "all men are created equal" was an expression that "excluded Negroes who were held in bondage, as well as the few who were free men."[3] This is a curious view, certainly one utterly incompatible with the intention of its author.

Writing 25 years after its publication, Thomas Jefferson made it clear for all to read that *all* men, irrespective of race, were included in the *Declaration*'s famous statement. He said:

> Because Sir Isaac Newton was superior to others in understanding, he was not therefore lord of the person or property of others. On this subject, they are gaining daily in the opinions of nations, and hopeful advances are making towards their [Negro] re-establishment on an equal footing with the other colors of the human family.[4]

When Jefferson wrote of equality in the *Declaration of Independence*, he understood that all men were not then living in that condition. He simply intended to declare what he considered to be a self-evident truth or what Abraham Lincoln later termed "a standard maxim for free society." In other words, equality was not where America began her existence but rather represented the *telos* or goal to which we fixed our destiny. To expect this revolution of man's historic condition to be completed at the same moment that it was announced in 1776 is to condemn the men of our founding for not being omnipotent. As long as a large body of Americans refused to consent to the principle of equality, Jefferson could only "declare the right, so that enforcement of it might follow as fast as circumstances should permit." Knowing the proneness of men to sacrifice their principles of justice for economic gain, he "left for them at least one hard nut to crack."[5]

In other words, the declaration of the principle of equality was an act of statesmanship, and statesmanship involves doing as much good as one can get away with. In this sense statesmanship becomes "removing the greatest amount of evil while disturbing the least amount of prejudice."[6] It is largely a *negative* art that demands the destruction of such evils as slavery, oppression, and civil discord.

The statesman's task, as Plato reminded us in *The Republic*, is chiefly that of the nurse or surgeon who has been charged with eliminating the diseases that plague the body politic. In a democratic republic this means that the statesman must instill in the citizenry eager consent to be its best self and make it feel that this is what it wanted all along. Because a democratic republic rests on popular opinion, the statesman must be a transcendent teacher and take the whole nation to school.[7] One of America's greatest statesmen, Abraham Lincoln, understood this when he observed: ". . . he who molds public sentiment goes deeper than he who enacts statutes and pronounces decisions. He makes statutes or decisions possible or impossible to execute."[8]

"Public opinion, on any subject, always has a 'central idea' from which all its minor thoughts radiate." The central idea that accompanied our founding, from which all minor thoughts radiated, was that "all men are created equal."

This was the teaching of Jefferson, which was later incorporated into the Constitution in the Bill of Rights and the addition of the Fourteenth Amendment in 1868. It extended the protection of rights and "equal protection of the laws" from the national to the state level of government.

To Jefferson the principle of equality was not only just but it was in his and every man's *enlightened self-interest* to pursue that justice lest there be "a revolution of the wheel of fortune." In his *Notes on the State of Virginia*, he prophetically warned those who refused to consent to the principle of equality:

> Indeed I tremble for my country when I reflect that God is just; that his justice cannot sleep forever; that considering numbers, nature and natural means only, a revolution of the wheel of fortune, an exchange of situation is among possible events; that it may become probable by supernatural interference! The Almighty has no attribute which can take side with us in such a contest.[9]

Given the ghetto riots of the late 1960s, the ascendance of groups like the Black Muslims, and the Black Panther "shoot-outs" in Chicago, Los Angeles, and Cleveland, no doubt many Americans must have thought that the revolutionary wheel was already spinning.

Thus *undemocratic means*—the conversion of ballots to bullets—toward the democratic end of equality produced more than 150 major riots in American cities between 1965 and 1968.[10]

Equality, however, is not the only principle enunciated in the *Declaration of Independence* or embodied in the Constitution. Linked to it is the principle that government derives its just powers from "the consent of the governed." The political cornerstone of a democracy is that the people are sovereign. The equality and liberty guaranteed in the *Declaration of Independence* and Constitution are ultimately in their hands; and, because unanimity is impossible in a nation as large as the United States, the pragmatic settlement of majority rule has obtained in every sizable democracy in the world. As Leslie Lipson has put it, "We count heads in order to avoid breaking them." [11]

Whereas during the 1960s some professed members of the Radical Left like H. Rap Brown and Jerry Rubin looked to equality as the "true" principle of American democracy and were willing to use undemocratic means, if necessary, to achieve their ends, many Conservatives attached themselves to what they considered to be the "true" principle of democracy, namely "consent of the governed" or what in modern parlance would be called freedom or liberty. In the words of one Conservative writer, Felix Morely, "Democracy, as the word is used in the United States, does not imply equality." [12] Likening equality to Marxian socialism, Morley insists that it spells the death of freedom and that socialism in this country "has been enormously helped by the Jeffersonian half-truth that 'all men are created equal'." [13]

The sad fact of American history, both past and present, is that a large body of Americans who have professed a love of freedom (at least their own) have refused to consent to their fellow American's demands for full equality, and, like their counterparts on the Radical Left, some have not been reluctant to use force to preserve their ideals.

White mobs, whether they be Southern lynching parties or Northern and Western rabble descending on black ghettos to kill indiscriminately any Negro who happened to cross their path, have punctuated American history with violence.[14] More frequently, however, white majorities have used *democratic means* to arrive at their *undemocratic ends*. By the ballot they have instituted Jim Crow segregation laws or, more recently, simply refused to consent to the equality demanded by the black minority. A prototype of the withdrawal of consent by a white majority occurred in the 1964 California elections when an overwhelming majority of the voters (4 million to 2 million) approved a state constitutional amendment sponsored by the California Real Estate Association to give absolute freedom to property owners to discriminate against prospective buyers or renters of their property on any basis, including race.[15] The U.S. Supreme Court subsequently ruled the California amendment unconstitutional in *Reitman v. Mulkev* (1967) because it was in direct conflict with the Fourteenth Amendment's guarantee to all of equal protection under the law.

No doubt the long history of the white majority's refusal to consent to the justice of black equality has prompted some Americans—black and white—to give up the idea of curative political reform in favor of surgical revolution. As one Negro intellectual has put it, the bourgeois-reformist Negroes "clutter up the Negro civil rights movement with their strident protests and really believe that American capitalism is going to *grant* them racial equality. . . ."[16]

The fact that the two democratic principles of liberty and equality found in the *Declaration of Independence* and the Constitution have not harmonized as well as the Founders intended accounts for much of the tragedy in American history as well as for the current politics of confrontation. Just such a confrontation took place before the Civil War when radical spokesmen like William Lloyd Garrison were making full demands for equality, whereas others like John C. Calhoun were pressing their full prerogatives for consent of the governed.

In times of crisis, like the Civil War and the racial strife of our own time, the struggle between the radical advocates of these two principles is magnified and permits the student of society to observe them with even greater clarity. In this sense the Civil War "is the most characteristic phenomenon in American politics, not because it represents statistical frequency, but because it represents the innermost character of that politics."[17]

The lessons of history clearly point to the necessity for statesmanship to harmonize the claims of consent with the claims of equality and that only when the politics of moderation replace the politics of confrontation can a wise resolution of this conflict become the basis of public policy.

Intrinsically, the two values of liberty and equality *are* compatible. They are merely two sides of the same coin. Democracy rests on the recognition of the dignity of the individual and the notion that the state exists for the individual rather than vice versa. The individual's place in society is basically a matter related to liberty, whereas the relation existing between those individuals in groups is essentially the concern of equality.

Thus liberty is concerned with the *individual* and equality appertains to the *group*. Yet freedom ends where injury to others begins. Would anyone seriously quarrel with Justice Oliver Wendall Holmes' celebrated opinion that rejected the freedom to shout falsely "fire!" in a crowded theater? True liberty is contingent on the freedom to do as everyone else does as well as the acceptance of the responsible use of that freedom. As Harry Jaffa has written, "the great engine of reason and conscience, in a free society, is the awareness that the freedom of each man, and his security from the abuses of power, consists precisely in the recognition that every other man is entitled to the same freedom, and the same security." [18]

Lincoln, of course, demonstrated in his famous debates with Stephen A. Douglas that both liberty and equality are based on the same principle of enlightened self-interest. His argument is worth recalling:

> If A. can prove, however conclusively, that he may, of right, enslave B.—why may not B. snatch the same argument, and prove equally, that he may enslave A?
>
> You say A. is white, and B. is black. It is *color,* then; the lighter having the right to rule the darker? Take care. By this rule, you are to be slave to the first man you meet, with a fairer skin than your own.
>
> You do not mean *color* exactly? You mean the whites are *intellectually* the superiors of the blacks; and therefore have the right to enslave them? Take care again. By this rule, you are to be slave to the first man you meet, with an intellect superior to your own.
>
> But, say you, it is a question of *interest;* and, if you can make it your *interest,* you have the right to enslave another. Very well. And if he can make it his interest, he has the right to enslave you.

Accordingly, liberty shades off into equality. With the Negro this is particularly true, for he is neither free to enter nor leave his race. As Professor Leslie Lipson has stated, "the connection between the problems of race relations and the principles of democracy is not primarily an issue of freedom. It is instead an issue of equality." [19] That liberty means nothing without equality was succinctly summed up by one Negro during the 1930s when he asserted that, "The first war was 'bout freedom and the war right after it [against Jim Crow segregation] was equalization." [20]

The Crisis in White Over Black

Gross inequalities ranging from the subordination of Negroes and women to the white male population to economic and educational deprivation of America's poor in the form of inadequate health care, housing, education, and unemployment have always existed in the United States. The broadening of the right to vote, to run for office, to have equal educational and employment opportunities, and to live wherever one chooses not only provides freedom for the individual in the particular realm in which it was hitherto absent but from a group point of view it also fosters equality.

Yet, as Aristotle pointed out in *The Politics*, equality may take two basic forms [21]—identical and proportional—and a political regime must choose between them, according to the precepts of justice. This is particularly true for a regime dedicated to the proposition that all men are created equal. What kind of equality is implied by that phrase? Identical or proportional?

In the first case equality means just what it says, namely, that men are "equal absolutely, and in all respects." [22] The other is an equality based on the ratio of effort among us, and that is necessarily unequal. Although the two forms of equality are by no means unrelated, identical equality has been the goal in American *political* life, whereas proportional equality has obtained in the *economic* and *social* sphere.

Identical political equality means that every sane adult citizen should have one vote and no more, as well as the same standing before the law. Considering the fact that the first 10 amendments were part of the original Constitution and that the Eighteenth and Twenty-first cancel each other (prohibition), the United States has added only 14 amendments to its Constitution in the last 185 years. Eight have broadened the suffrage from white males over the age of 21 with enough property to meet the state voting requirements to the present condition in which all citizens over the age of 18 are entitled to vote, irrespective of race, color, previous condition of servitude, sex, and property status or if they happen to live in the nation's capital.

This is not to say that the law has always been respected. All too often white majorities, North and South/East and West, stood on common ground in denying the Negro political equality. *De facto* or *de jure* segregation, it was all the same . . . and behind it stood state enforcement and, ultimately, white violence. Whereas the South used Jim Crow legislation to require Negroes to use grossly unequal facilities in schools, transportation, housing, and recreation, the rest of the country did the same thing with residential segregation ordinances, restrictive covenants in deeds that forbade the sale of property to Negroes, and discriminatory employment practices, thereby institutionalizing black ghettos, which cut off black America from its more affluent white counterpart. Politically, economic deprivation was an effective check in all parts of America on the black minority in deterring it from voting. When that failed, violence was always a ready alternative.

The Southern style leaned toward lynching, a rather amorphous term which most commonly took the form of hanging but which also included a broader range of illegal violent acts. Between 1882 and 1946 Southern lynching accounted for no less than 83 percent of the 3425 Negroes murdered during that period.[23]

The rest of the country indulged more in race riots, though white majorities were not exempt from a little lynching of their own. Indeed, only a few months after Negro soldiers returned home from the battlegrounds of World War I, where they had fought to "make the world safe for democracy," they found that democracy in America was in itself none too safe for black Americans, for approximately 25 white-instigated race riots, which broke out in American urban centers, ushered in "the greatest period of interracial strife the nation had ever witnessed."[24]

In contrast to the racial strife of the late 1960s, which began
in the ghetto rather than as an assault from without, black Americans then typically made little or no attempt to defend themselves
from the white-originated violence that indiscriminately killed any
available member of the black community. In the words of one
scholar, the

> . . . killing of Negroes was indiscriminate. . . . Some of those
> who lost their lives were among the oldest and most respected
> colored people in the city. Most Negroes in the riot zone
> made no attempts to defend themselves, and the small
> number of casualties among the whites clearly showed the
> one-sidedness of the riot.[25]

American politics has been punctuated with periods of stagnation
in the march to redeem the promise of equality in the *Declaration
of Independence*. This was especially true in the era of Jim Crow
segregation (1863–1954),[26] when black Americans were denied their
identical political equality in voting and holding office by such
nefarious devices as white violence, white primaries, racial gerrymandering, poll taxes, "literacy" tests, and other discriminatory voting
requirements.

Jim Crow began to wane as a result of the Great Depression in
the 1930s and America's resistance to the virulent racism of Nazi
Germany during the 1940s. Out of this emerged the welfare state
which placed limits on economic inequality by means of such programs as social security, welfare, and the progressive income tax
and renewed the country's commitments to the principle of identical
political equality.

One by one the impediments to political equality have been
declared unconstitutional by the Supreme Court or prohibited by
the Congress. Employing the Fourteenth and Fifteenth Amendments,
which guarantee equal protection of the law to all Americans and
prohibit the states from depriving black Americans of the right to
vote, the Court in 1944 found the Southern white primary unconstitutional,[27] forbade racial gerrymandering in 1960,[28] and invalidated
the use of poll taxes to keep people from voting in 1966.[29] The
Voting Rights Act of 1965 mandated that no person may be denied
the right to vote because of inability to read or write English if

evidence is provided that one has successfully completed the equivalent of a sixth-grade education in an accredited school within the jurisdiction of the United States.

The Voting Rights Act of 1965 was especially significant in reducing the gap between theory and practice as far as identical political equality is concerned by preventing Southern whites from refusing to consent to Negro voting. That Act provided for direct federal action to help black Americans register and vote, thus avoiding the protracted legal suits that have accompanied Negro efforts to get on the voting rolls when it was handled at the state level by white state officials. The success in providing Southern Negroes with their right to participate equally with white citizens in politics can be seen in the report of the U.S. Commission on Civil Rights.

Moreover, the Court, in its reapportionment decisions of the 1960s, has moved to make each vote carry the same *weight* by eliminating population discrepancies in state and federal legislative districts which underrepresented Americans living in cities in general and black Americans in particular. Although 87 percent of the black population lived in the rural South in 1900, today about 73 percent of the 21.5 million black Americans live in metropolitan areas and almost half of them outside the South.

This is largely the result of a black migration which reached flood tide during and between World Wars I and II, when black sharecroppers and tenant farmers were pushed off the land, first by the cotton boll weevil and then by the expansion and movement westward of commercial agriculture during and after the 1940s. At the same time they were being drawn into the cities of the North and West by the labor shortages created by both wars. The *American Negro Reference Book* estimates that no less than 3 million black people left the South between 1916 and 1930 and that migration has not abated to the present day. With this exodus the racial problem of the United States changed from a rural "Southern problem" to an urban national concern.

Not only have Negroes moved into America's metropolitan centers at an unprecedented rate but the black population has been growing faster than its white counterpart. Thus, whereas 1 of every 10 Americans was black in 1950, in 1973 1 of every 8 was a Negro. This statistical fact, coupled with the exodus of the white population from

VOTING REGISTRATION FIGURES BY RACE—ELEVEN SOUTHERN STATES

	Spring 1968				November 1964		
	White Registered	Negro Registered	% of Voting Age Whites Registered	% of Voting Age Negroes Registered		Negro Registered	% of Voting Age Negroes Registered
Alabama	1,212,317	248,432	89.6	51.6		111,000	23.0
Arkansas	616,000	121,000	72.4	62.8		105,000	54.4
Florida	2,131,105	299,033	81.4	63.6		300,000	63.7
Georgia	1,443,630	322,496	80.3	52.6		270,000	44.0
Louisiana	1,200,617	303,148	93.1	58.9		164,700	32.0
Mississippi	639,066	181,233	91.5	59.8		28,500	6.7
North Carolina	1,602,980	277,404	83.0	51.3		258,000	46.8
South Carolina	731,096	190,017	81.7	51.2		144,000	38.8
Tennessee	1,434,000	225,000	80.6	71.7		218,000	69.4
Texas	2,600,000	400,000	53.3	61.6		375,000	57.7
Virginia	1,140,000	243,000	63.4	55.6		200,000	45.7
Regional Total	14,750,811	2,810,763	76.5	57.2		2,174,200	43.3

Source: U.S. Commission on Civil Rights, Voter Education Project of the Southern Regional Council

the cities to the suburbs, has made the Negro American more of an urban dweller than the white, with about 73 percent of all Negroes living in metropolitan areas compared with 70 percent of the whites.[30]

The net result is that Negroes now constitute a disproportionately high percentage of the population in the nation's largest cities. Indeed, a large number of cities during the 1970s will come close to having black majorities, despite the fact that the total Negro proportion of the national population is only about 12 percent. During this decade, according to the projections of the *Congressional Quarterly*, Negroes will rapidly approach a numerical majority in many of the nation's *largest* cities and already constitute 40 percent or more of the population in 14 major cities, including Washington, Richmond, Gary, Baltimore, Detroit, Newark, St. Louis, New Orleans, and Trenton.[31]

As a reflection of these population trends, as well as the "one man, one vote" principle enunciated in the reapportionment cases,[32] Negroes have been more successful in winning political office. By the opening of the decade of the 1970s not only had Negro suffrage dramatically broadened but black Americans had served in the Cabinet, on the Supreme Court, in the Senate, and in House of Representatives. Moreover, black mayors had been elected in many of the nation's largest cities and an estimated 1,860 Negroes were serving as elected government officials throughout the country.[33] This is not to say that Negroes are proportionately represented in public office. They are not. Though they constitute nearly 12 percent of the population, they hold less than one-half of one percent of the more than half-million elected offices in the country. Nonetheless, the increase in voter registration and turnout, as well as the number of black public officials, is evidence that the United States has again begun to move toward the realization of identical political equality.

Even the economic and social goal of proportional equality is coming closer to approximation. We all understand the meaning of this form of equality, for it is the basis of our federal income tax. Instead of the rich and the poor helping to defray the cost of government by paying an identical *per annum* tax, each is required to contribute according to his ability on a graduating tax rate as he becomes wealthier.

Beginning with President Harry S. Truman's Executive Order,

which integrated the armed forces in 1948, 20 million black Americans who had been largely excluded from American society by Jim
Crow segregation were started on the road to equal opportunity
in education, employment, housing, transportation, and public accommodations.

Richard Wright describes the hopelessness and resignation that
characterized the black portion of our population during the Jim
Crow period when inequities were so great that they generated
nothing but despair. In *Uncle Tom's Children,* he writes:

> My Jim Crow education continued on the next job, which
> was portering in a clothing store. One morning, while polish-
> ing brass out front, the boss and his twenty-year old son got
> out of their car and half dragged and half kicked a Negro
> woman into the store. A policeman standing at the corner
> looked on, twirling his night stick. I watched out of the corner
> of my eye, never slackening the strokes of my chamois upon
> the brass. After a few minutes, I heard shrill screams coming
> from the rear of the store. Later the woman stumbled out,
> bleeding, crying, and holding her stomach. When she reached
> the end of the block, the policeman grabbed her and accused
> her of being drunk. Silently, I watched him throw her into
> a patrol wagon.
>
> When I went to the rear of the store, the boss and his
> son were washing their hands at the sink. They were chuck-
> ling. The floor was bloody and strewn with wisps of hair and
> clothing. No doubt I must have appeared pretty shocked, for
> the boss slapped me reassuringly on the back.
>
> "Boy, that's what we do to niggers when they don't want
> to pay their bills," he said, laughing.

Later that day Wright told his fellow Negro porters of the incident.
No one seemed surprised, and one injected:

> Huh! Is tha' all thêy did t' her? Shucks! Man, she's a lucky
> bitch! . . . Hell, it's a wonder they didn't lay her when they
> got through.[34]

Richard Wright's Jim Crow education, of course, included much
more than this experience. Second-class citizenship and the segregation of white and black people in public and private facilities had

been constitutionally sanctioned since 1896, when the Supreme Court upheld such practices under the "separate but equal" doctrine of *Plessy v. Ferguson.*[35] Dissenting in that opinion, Associate Justice John Marshall Harlan declared that the Constitution was "color-blind" and that "the thin disguise of equal accommodations will not mislead anyone nor atone for the wrong done this day."

A step was taken toward atonement 58 years later, in 1954, when a unanimous Supreme Court knocked down the "separate but equal" doctrine in *Brown v. Topeka Board of Education.*[36] Writing the opinion for the Court, Chief Justice Earl Warren stated that "the doctrine of 'separate but equal' has no place" in American life because "separate educational facilities are inherently unequal."

During the same decade Jim Crow was dealt another blow when the Supreme Court outlawed segregation on interstate motor carriers.[37] In 1960 it completely unhinged Jim Crow in interstate travel by ruling that segregated bus stations—even though not owned by the interstate carrier—also violated the constitutional right to equal protection of the law, guaranteed by the Fourteenth Amendment and implemented by the Interstate Commerce Act.[38]

Even as the gap between American democratic theory and practice was being reduced in these areas groups like the Congress of Racial Equality (CORE) and the National Association for the Advancement of Colored People (NAACP) were testing Southern compliance to them. The resistance encountered by the "Freedom Riders" in Montgomery, Alabama, in 1961, the murder of NAACP leader Medgar Evers in 1963, the bombing of the Sixteenth Street Baptist Church which killed four Negro girls in Birmingham in the same year, the murder of white civil rights worker Mrs. Viola Liuzzo by three members of the Ku Klux Klan in 1965, and the 1968 assassination of Nobel laureate Dr. Martin Luther King—the undisputed leader of the nonviolent arm of the Negro movement for equality—demonstrated that Southern White consent to black equality and the death of Jim Crow would not come without agony.

Nonetheless, the black American did make significant gains during the 1950s and 60s, albeit most of those victories were won in the *cities* of the *South* and affected only the *middle-class* Negro. Largely excluded were the poor Negroes of the North and West and those who remained in the small villages of the South.

Spurred by groups like the NAACP and CORE and stimulated by the realities of Cold War politics, which silhouetted the incongruity of America courting new black nations in Africa to prevent them from turning to Communism while neglecting its own black population at home, Congress in 1957 passed a mild Civil Rights Act. It was the first such law since 1875; it prohibited interference with the right to vote and created a Commission on Civil Rights to make reports on discrimination and the equal protection of the laws to all American citizens.

On the eve of the commemoration of the Emancipation Centennial in 1963 Birmingham police chief Bull Connor inadvertently stimulated further civil rights legislation by his ruthless smashing of a nonviolent antisegregation campaign headed by Martin Luther King with clubs, police dogs, and electric cow prodders. A wave of national sympathy and support—heightened by the assassination of President John F. Kennedy in November—led in 1964 to the passage of the strongest civil rights act in American history.

Obtaining consent for the principle of equality which permeates this act involved a bitter struggle in the Senate to invoke a two-thirds vote of cloture to end a 57-day Southern filibuster against the bill. On June 10 the Senate succeeded for the first time in its history in obtaining cloture against a civil rights filibuster in a vote so close that all 100 Senators were present and voting, including the dying California Democrat Clair Engle who had to be carried to the floor of the Senate after having twice undergone brain surgery for cancer.[39]

Under the provisions of the Civil Rights Act of 1964 Congress prohibited discrimination in public accommodations (restaurants, hotels, theaters, etc.) engaged in interstate commerce or owned by public authorities. To enforce the law Congress created a Fair Employment Practices Commission (FEPC) and empowered the President to cut off federal funds for programs in which racial discrimination was present.

While these civil rights laws were taking effect in the late 1960s a wave of ghetto violence spread across the nation. Frustrated by unemployment rates that reached as high as 42 percent in some cities, by rat-infested and overcrowded housing, by decaying schools, by distrust of the police who sometimes used double standards of justice for black and white, and relatively unaffected and unimproved by the civil rights legislation of the 1960s, Northern and Western blacks exploded in urban centers from Newark and Harlem to Detroit and Watts. All the riots were touched off, according to the U.S. Riot Commission Report, by minor incidents involving the police.[40]

Yet ironically the very violence of the 1960s may be indicative of the hope that progress toward the ideal of equality had generated. Gross inequalities have always existed in the United States, but when such inequities are most intense they produce a type of melancholy fatalism born of despair. Alexis de Tocqueville long ago noted:

> The hatred that men bear to privilege increases in proportion as privileges become fewer and less considerable, so that democratic passions would seem to burn most fiercely just when they have the least fuel.[41]

Crane Brinton's *Anatomy of Revolution* confirmed this observation more recently when he maintained that prerevolutionary society is characterized by relative prosperity and growing social equality.[42]

The result of the urban violence, however, was to polarize race relations in the United States. When H. Rap Brown declared that violence is "as American as cherry pie" and the civil rights movement seemed to shift from the nonviolent sit-ins of Martin Luther King to the "Black Power" movement of Stokely Carmichael and Eldridge Cleaver, fear of urban violence and crime seemed to skyrocket in America.[43]

Although the prospects of a racial revolution in America are remote,[44] the fear of racial violence played a strong role in the election of Richard Nixon to the presidency in 1968. Sensing perfectly the "silent majority's" fear of racial riots after the orgy of violence that exploded during the long hot summers of the mid-1960s, Nixon defined the social issue of that election by raising the specter of "sirens in the night" in answer to calls from "cities enveloped in smoke and flame." Indeed, when President Nixon and Vice President Agnew spoke of the "silent majority" taking over the country in 1970, public opinion analyst Lou Harris reported that his surveys indicated that if such a mythical majority existed that about the only glue holding it together was "a common aversion to what is presumably the vocal minority" which consists of the black population concentrated largely in the South and in the large urban centers "who had the audacity to say that they wanted 'Equality Now.' "[45]

That aversion has taken many forms but none more emotional

than the storm over busing as a means of integrating public schools. Whereas the *Brown* decision dealt squarely with the *de jure* segregation in the 17 states that required segregated schools by law, it did not deal with *de facto* segregation in neighborhood public schools that was largely the result of segregated residential patterns.

That *de jure* segregation is widespread has been thoroughly documented by the 1966 Coleman Report (*Equality of Educational Opportunity*) and the Civil Rights Commission's *Racial Isolation in the Public Schools*. The Coleman group, after surveying teachers, administrators, and students in 4000 public schools, found that "almost 80 percent of all Negro pupils in the first grade attend schools that are between 90 and 100 percent Negro. . . . In the South, most students attend schools that are 100 percent white or Negro. . . ." The study then went on to report that such segregated schools educationally deprived *both* black and white children in America, for evidence suggests that minority children learn faster when there is racial integration of classrooms and that, far from damaging educational opportunity for whites, white pupils have either gained or stayed at about the same level after integration.[46]

Focusing on this problem in 1968, the Supreme Court held that school systems had to convert to "unitary," or single, systems without racial division and called for a school system in which there would be no white or black schools "but just schools." It said, "The burden on a school board today is to come forward with a plan that promises realistically to work, and promises realistically to work *now*." In 1971, in the *Charlotte-Mecklenburg* case, the Court held unanimously that busing is *a* proper means of desegregating schools.

It must be emphasized that the Court did *not* order wholesale busing but rather sanctioned it as *one* reasonable tool. Despite the care with which the Court took in this decision, busing drew a violent reaction during 1970 and 1971 when it began dominating national headlines in the wake of incidents in Lamar, South Carolina, Denver, Colorado, and Pontiac, Michigan, where school buses were overturned and burned. Adding fuel to the fire, President Nixon took to national TV in 1972 to condemn school busing for having reached "massive" and unreasonable proportions and to urge a "moratorium" on all busing until the passage of his Equal Opportunities Educational Act which holds multiple attractions for those who would like to dodge school integration. Among other things it provides that no busing may be ordered by a court "until it is demonstrated by clear and convincing evidence" that "no other method set out in Section 402 [of this act] will provide an adequate remedy." Another method, spelled out in Section 402 as "the construction of new schools," has led some to fear that Nixon's Equal Opportunities Educational Act would lead back to the "separate but equal" doctrine of the Jim Crow era.[47]

President Nixon's charge that busing has reached a stage of "massive" proportions does not square with the evidence. His own Secretary of Transportation John A. Volpe, quoting the National Highway Traffic Safety Administration, estimates that less than 1 percent of the annual increase in busing can be attributed to desegregation.[48] Moreover, school busing did not become a controversial issue in this country until it involved mixing white with black, affluent with poor. As one outraged white parent put it, "As long as we don't have niggers on there, it's not busing. Busing is making white children get on with niggers."[49]

The "massive" busing of children for desegregation purposes, which President Nixon declaimed in his 1972 TV address, beclouded more than clarified the issue. The U.S. Commission on Civil Rights itself estimates that this kind of school transportation has increased less than 3 percent of the total busing of children since the *Brown* decision, whereas the percentage of bused school children for other purposes has increased almost 45 percent. All of this points to the inescapable conclusion that busing historically has been regarded by parents as an advantage. It is only when it involves desegregation that it becomes controversial.

In response to the steady increase in enrollments and school consolidations that replaced the old one- and two-room schools, busing of public school children has spread rapidly over the years. Since 1921 the number of children transported in school buses has risen from 600,000 to nearly 20,000,000.[50] For almost as long as there has been automotive transportation American children have been going to school by bus at public expense and almost always that busing has been regarded by their parents as an advantage that allowed their children to attend a superior consolidated school or special classes for gifted or disadvantaged children. Indeed, black children in the South were rarely if ever provided bus transportation, but white children were carried clear across town to their all white schools with the blessing of their approving parents.[51] As the U.S. Civil Rights Commission put it:

> To grasp the importance of the school bus to American education, one needs only to imagine the national outcry that would result if all bus service for all purposes suddenly were withdrawn. Only when busing is used for desegregation purposes is there bitter complaint.[52]

Conclusion

Thus busing has served to conceal the real issue, which is not the new "yellow peril" in the form of school buses. Busing of white children to superior schools or for the purpose of segregation has long been a familiar feature of American life. The real issue is whether our nation will remain, as the U.S. Riot Commission found it in 1968, "two societies, one black, one white—separate and unequal." [53]

To unite the nation will require movement toward the redemption of the promises of liberty and equality as they are found in the *Declaration of Independence* and the Constitution. What is needed is enlightened public opinion, one that understands the necessity of fusing, or at least balancing, the principles of liberty with those of equality. The very foundation of democratic government rests on an acceptance of the necessity of a rational society, one that has the requisite moral virtue and intelligence to rule itself well. It is for that reason that self-government is best understood not only as government by consent but also as *self-mastery* by bridling passion to reason.

Because self-mastery is not always in bountiful supply, it is the task of the statesman to elevate and instruct public opinion to behave in a manner that is good both for the individual and the nation. To fail in this task is to run the risk that the dangerous gap between two societies—one black, one white—will grow even wider.

Notes

1. John Hope Franklin, "The Bitter Years of Slavery," *Life* (November 22, 1968), 108; for a rebuttal to Professor Franklin's arguments see Fred R. Mabbutt, "The Bitter Years Of Slavery: A Response to the arguments of John Hope Franklin," University of Houston *Forum* (Fall-Winter, 1970), 13–18.

2. Roy P. Basler, Ed., *The Collected Works of Abraham Lincoln* (New Brunswick, New Jersey: Rutgers University Press, 1953), III, p. 375.

3. Otto Kerner et al., *Report Of The National Advisory Commission On Civil Disorders* (New York: Bantam, 1968), p. 207.

4. Adrienne Koch and William Peden, Eds., *The Life and Selected Writings of Thomas Jefferson* (New York: Modern Library, 1944), p. 595.

5. *The Collected Works of Abraham Lincoln,* II, pp. 405–406.

6. Morton J. Frisch and Richard G. Stevens, Eds., *American Political Thought: The Philosophic Dimensions of American Statesmanship* (New York: Scribner's, 1971), p. 6.

7. *Ibid.,* p. 20.

8. Harry V. Jaffa, "Expediency and Morality in The Lincoln-Douglas Debates," *The Anchor Review,* No. 2 (1957), 177–204.

9. Thomas Jefferson, *Notes on the State of Virginia,* Query XVIII (Chapel Hill: University of North Carolina Press, 1955), p. 163.

10. Thomas R. Dye, *The Politics of Equality* (Indianapolis: Bobbs-Merrill, 1971), p. 176.

11. Leslie Lipson, *The Democratic Civilization* (London: Oxford University Press, 1964), p. 551.

12. Felix Morely, *Freedom and Federalism* (Chicago: Henry Regnery Company, 1959), p. 11. Morley makes a subtle distinction between freedom and liberty, defining the former as "essentially an absence of external restraint" and the latter "as a more positive condition, involving a measure of personal choice which is less inherent in freedom."

13. *Ibid.,* p. 49.

14. John Hope Franklin, *From Slavery To Freedom* (New York: Knopf, 1969), pp. 477–497.

15. For Congressional action in the area of open housing see *Revolution in Civil Rights, 1945–1968* (Washington, D.C., Congressional Quarterly, 1968), 84–91.

16. Harold Cruse, found in Lennox S. Hinds, "The Relevance of the Past to the Present: A Political Interpretation," in *Black Life and Culture in the United States* (New York: Crowell, 1971), p. 365. [Emphasis mine.]

17. Harry V. Jaffa, *Equality and Liberty* (New York: Oxford University Press, 1965), p. vii; see also Harry V. Jaffa, *Crisis of the House Divided* (Garden City, New York: Doubleday, 1959).

18. Harry V. Jaffa, " 'Value Consensus' in Democracy: The Issue in the Lincoln-Douglas Debates," *American Political Science Review,* LII (1958), 751.

19. Leslie Lipson, *The Democratic Civilization,* p. 95.

20. Allen Weinstein and Frank Otto Gatell, Ed., *The Segregation Era: 1963-1954* (New York: Oxford University Press, 1970), p. vii.

21. Ernest Barker, Ed., *The Politics of Aristotle* (London: Oxford University Press, 1968), Book V, pp. 204-205.

22. *Ibid.,* p. 204.

23. See *1952 Negro Year Book* (Tuskegee, Alabama: Tuskegee Institute, 1952), p. 278.

24. Franklin, *From Slavery to Freedom,* p. 480.

25. Ellito M. Rudwick, *Race Riot at East St. Louis* (Carbondale, Illinois: Southern Illinois University Press, 1964), p. 53.

26. C. Vann Woodward notes that this racial caste system was born in the ante-bellum North and reached an advanced stage before moving South in force after the Civil War. The 1954 Supreme Court ruling in *Brown v. Board of Education* made such a system unconstitutional. See C. Van Woodward, *The Strange Career of Jim Crow* (New York: Oxford University Press, 1966), p. 17.

27. *Smith v. Allwright* (1944) 321 U.S. 649.

28. *Gomillion v. Lightfoot* (1960) 364 U.S. 339.

29. *Harper v. Virginia Board of Education* (1966) 338 U.S. 663.

30. "Trends in Negro Urban Population," *Revolution in Civil Rights,* pp. 116-119.

31. *Ibid.*

32. See *Baker v. Carr* (1962) 369 U.S. 186; *Reynolds v. Sims* (1964) 377 U.S. 533; *Wesberry v. Sanders* (1964) 376 U.S. 1.

33. "Black Politics: New Way to Overcome," *Newsweek* (June 7, 1971), 30-39.

34. Richard Wright, *Uncle Tom's Children* (New York: Harper-Row, 1938), p. 6.

35. *Plessy v. Ferguson* (1896) 163 U.S. 537.

36. *Brown v. Board of Education of Topeka Kansas* (1955) 349 U.S. 394.

37. *Henderson v. United States* (1950) 339 U.S. 816.

38. *Boynton v. United States* (1960).

39. "The Congress," *Time* (June 19, 1964), pp. 15-18.

40. *Report of the National Advisory Commission on Civil Disorders,* p. 206.

41. Alexis de Tocqueville, *Democracy in America,* II (New York: Vintage, 1945), p. 312.

42. Clarence Crane Brinton, *The Anatomy of Revolution* (New York: Vintage, 1965), especially chapter 9.

43. Richard M. Scammon and Ben J. Wattenberg, *The Real Majority* (New York: Coward, McCann & Geoghegan, 1970), pp. 17, 21, 40-41, 180, 207-208.

44. Barrington Moore, Jr., "Revolution in America?" *The New York Review* (January 30, 1969), 6–12.

45. Public address by Louis Harris, Pepperdine College Forum (Los Angeles, California), April 20, 1970.

46. James Coleman et al., *Equality of Educational Opportunity* (Washington, D.C.: National Center for Educational Statistics, U.S. Office of Education, 1966).

47. I. F. Stone, "Moving the Constitution to the Back of the Bus," *The New York Review* (April 20, 1972), 4–11.

48. U.S. Commission on Civil Rights, "Your Child and Busing" (Washington, D.C.: U.S. Commission on Civil Rights, May 1972), p. 7.

49. Neil Maxwell, *Wall Street Journal* (March 20, 1972).

50. "Your Child and Busing," p. 7.

51. *Ibid.*, pp. 7–9; "The Agony of Busing Moves North," *Time* (November 15, 1971), 57–64.

52. "Your Child and Busing," p. 8.

53. *Report of the National Advisory Commission on Civil Disorders*, p. 1.

FROM FIVE . . .

The first Women's Rights Convention met at Seneca Falls, New York, in July 1848 and drafted a manifesto modeled on the Declaration of Independence. "We hold these truths to be self-evident," states the proclamation, "that all men and women are created equal." Elizabeth Cady Stanton, Lucretia Mott, and other feminists of the mid-nineteenth century demanded fulfillment of the promise of political equality contained in the Declaration. In so doing they stirred the American political cauldron until womankind was enfranchised by the passage of the Nineteenth Amendment in 1920. A half-century later "feminist ferment" is again a prominent part of our political landscape.

. . . ON TO SIX

SIX

FEMINIST FERMENT AND THE MYTH OF THE AMERICAN WOMAN

FRED R. MABBUTT

Voltaire once asserted, "History is nothing but a pack of tricks that we play upon the dead." Although this judgment can be viewed with considerable skepticism, it nonetheless must be admitted that the writing of history is a tricky business. Nowhere is this more true than in the academician's treatment of women in American history. Although such an assertion is often received with shock and indignation in academic circles, it should hardly be considered a startling revelation, especially when we consider that nearly all our history is written by men whose ideas largely reflect the dominant white-male culture of American society.[1]

The net result has been that American historians either ignore women entirely, or worse, they submerge their manuscripts in unchallenged prejudice or mythology which assumes that women shrewdly control and manipulate the property of men or are capable of little more than childbearing and homemaking. One need not go far enough to agree with Arthur Schopenhauer's opinion that Clio, the muse of history, "is as permeated with lies as a street-whore with syphilis,"[2] to recognize that women in American history are at best a shadowy subject.

At one extreme it is possible to measure the American historical tradition of feminine neglect by perusing the pages of Samuel Eliot Morison's *The Oxford History of the American People*. In that prestigious tome so significant an event as the doubling of the American electorate by the enfranchisement of women (the Nineteenth Amendment) rates a bare two sentences in a section entitled "Boot-Legging and Other Sports."[3] At the other extreme the historical mythology of women is rampant and may be found in even the best of America's scholars.

Henry Steele Commager, for example, reassuringly tells us in *The American Mind* that the hand that rocks the cradle controls the wealth of America and has converted the United States into a veritable matriarchy.

> Twentieth-century America, even more than nineteenth, seemed to be a woman's country. The supremacy of women could be read in the statistics of property ownership, insurance, education, or literature, or in the advertisements of any popular magazine.

This is a far-reaching conclusion to draw, especially in lieu of the facts that 8 of every 10 welfare recipients in our largest cities are women, that women as a whole are paid only about 58 percent as much as men, that the property owner deeds and insurance policies that Professor Commager is reading are in reality tax loopholes used by men to avoid taxes or wealth inherited by women *from* deceased husbands (usually well after their sixtieth birthday), and that women as a group probably control no more than 15 to 20 percent of our national wealth.[5]

Elsewhere the historian's lack of empathy or outright arrogance has produced a history of women both lacking in understanding and credible analysis. Professor Ruth Rosen has drawn attention to Page Smith's introduction in his new book, *Daughters of a Promised Land,* to demonstrate this point. In that introduction, Professor Smith writes:

> The writing of this book owes nothing to my wife. She viewed the whole enterprise with undisguised skepticism, interrupted me frequently to ask if the Joneses would make good dinner partners with the Browns or whether the Thompsons will go with the Johnsons, seduced me from my labors with delicious meals (so that my girth grew with my book) and, most unnerving of all, said periodically, "How you could pretend to know anything about women . . . !" Which of course I don't.[6]

Professor Smith "then goes on to prove this ignorance in the following three hundred and ninety-two pages."[7]

With such hoary mythmaking it is difficult to ascertain the role of women in America's past. Yet we must make the effort if we hope to understand the present and make intelligent decisions about the future.

The Differential Impact of History and the American Woman

Unconsciously historians have made generalizations about the American people based on the assumption "that since American men are dominant, the characteristics of American men are the characteristics of the American people."[8] Such "shakey" logic has quite literally resulted in half-truths or conclusions that even run counter to historical reality.

David Potter has suggested that the famous frontier thesis of Frederick Jackson Turner is a notable example of this kind of historical reasoning. Turner's argument, it will be recalled, was that free land on the American frontier afforded the American people unprecedented economic opportunity to break away from the sociopolitical hammerlock of the Old World to become more individualistic and egalitarian in their daily lives.[9]

Although it is true that the frontier did allow men greater individualism and economic opportunity, it is not true that it provided women with "a gate of escape from the bondage of the past." Women did not share in the economic benefits of fur trapping, breaking virgin soil, herding cattle, or prospecting for gold because these economic pursuits were largely barred to them by both social convention and law. Rather than becoming more individualistic, most women became more subordinate to the men on whom they depended for protection and performance of the back-breaking tasks demanded by a pioneer existence. In such a frontier setting, in which a heavy premium was necessarily placed on brute strength and fearlessness, the man acted as the producer of raw materials needed by the family, and "his woman," as an unequal partner in a patriarchal family relationship, served as the processor of those materials into preserved foodstuffs, soaps, candles, and clothing.[10]

Thus the frontier had a differential impact on the sexes. In the agrarian-subsistence economy of the frontier the family had to be a functional economic unit. In the social structure, shaped though not determined by the frontier, men no doubt did experience greater freedom and economic opportunity than in the crowded cities of the East, but women had neither economic nor political standing in any section of the country and the western frontier was anything but conducive to female individualism and egalitarianism. As one frontier aphorism summed it up: "This country is all right for men and dogs, but it's hell on women and horses."[11] For women individualism and economic opportunity "began pretty much where the frontier left off"—in the cities.

Only in the urban setting did women have an opportunity to elevate their status and gain a better position in society's division of labor. Whereas women on the frontier had been confined to the unpaid economic and biological role of *Kinder, Küche, Kirche,* the dynamics of urban industrial growth brought ever-increasing numbers of women into factories as paid wage earners. Although this process initiated a barbarous capitalistic exploitation of women in those factories, it also brought women into the same orbit with men in the cities where they also were wage earners. In a society that measures status in terms of income and occupation this development represented the first female bridgehead in the battle of women to win for themselves the virtues that Frederick Jackson Turner extolled in his Frontier Thesis.

In the rise of manufacturing during and after the War of 1812 women not only left their homes for wages in the textile mills and booteries of the Atlantic seaboard but they also found less to do at home as they discovered that it was cheaper and easier to buy their foodstuffs, candles, soaps, and clothing from stores than to manufacture them themselves.[12] Women, in the view of many men, were challenging their pre-eminent position as it existed under the old agrarian morality, but the price was worth it, for females had now become an investment rather than a consumer appendage, "a source of wealth, rather than an incumbrance."[13]

Just as the frontier had had a differential effect on the sexes, so too did the urban processes of industrialization and municipal growth. In the city a greater economic leveling between the sexes obtained as machinery replaced the muscle power that had subordinated women to a position of dependency on men on the frontier. Now the premium was on labor costs and the ability to adapt to industrial technology. Because women represented a cheap pool of labor, their economic status was elevated for the first time to the level of a quasi-independent wage earner. At the same time the role of men was reduced from that of frontier "producer" to urban wage earner and their individualism suffered from the same regimentation in the factories as that experienced by women. Thus a rough—though procrustean—equality between the sexes, which had been absent on the frontier, existed in the cities.

This is not to say that women in the cities were suddenly emancipated from their surordination to men or liberated from social and economic injustice. Far from it. Women often worked in factories for less pay than men, though they performed the same tasks. It does not mean, however, that all women who worked in the cities experienced the same hardships or the same uplift. As Professor Mary Lynn has suggested, great differences existed between native-born women who worked in American factories during our early period of industrialization and the immigrant women and girls who increasingly replaced them after 1840.

The farmer's daughters who spent two or three years before
marriage in the mills of New England did experience a considerable expansion of their economic and social freedom, and
factory life for them offered lighter work, shorter hours, and
higher wages than did staying on the family farm. But speed-
ups, wage cuts, and the recruitment of immigrants who would
work for subsistence wages changed the situation. It is the
later women who had the double burden of work and family.

For them female emancipation could begin only after the twin
burdens of employment and family life were lessened. As Gerda
Lerner has pointed out: "It was only *after* economic and technological
advances made housework an obsolete occupation, only *after* technological and medical advances made all work physically easier and
childbearing no longer an inevitable yearly burden on women, that
emancipation of women could begin." [14]

It is clear, then, that the advances did not accrue to women
uniformly as a group. Class, income, and race were far more important than sex in determining leisure. The only women who profited
from America's industrial revolution belonged to the white middle
class; only they acquired the leisure time to spend in feminist agita-
tion. Most of the rest of womankind was far too preoccupied with
survival.

One major reason for the precipitation of feminist discontent after
1830 was the cognizance by these middle-class white women that
much of the freedom they enjoyed during the colonial and early
American periods was evaporating as Victorian notions of domesticity
resulted in an ideological belief system that forced them out of
business and the professions. In one sense nineteenth-century feminism can be viewed as a result of the frustrated expectations of white
middle-class women. It is no accident that the feminists of 1848,
who held the first Women's Rights Convention of Seneca Falls, were
with few exceptions like their heirs in the women's liberation movement of the 1970s—white, middle-class, well-educated, and urban-
based.

In contrast to some of the feminine furies of the contemporary
women's liberation movement, the feminist movement of the late
nineteenth- and early twentieth-centuries was conservative, bent not
so much on transforming the structure of American society as getting

into it. Although it began radically enough in the nineteenth century by interlocking with a spectrum of social reforms ranging from the abolition of slavery to public education and temperance, the women's rights movement gradually retrenched after the Civil War to a suffragist movement and the mouthpiece of white, middle-class feminism.

Crucial in this transformation, as W. L. O'Neill points out in *Everyone Was Brave*, was the failure of nineteenth-century feminists to come to grips with the issue of marriage and the family. With the possible exception of Susan B. Anthony and Elizabeth Cady Stanton before the Woodhull-Beecher scandal and Charlotte Perkins Gilman in the 1890s feminists were reluctant to confront the family as a question, viewing it as far too threatening for their era. To most Victorians—indeed to most contemporary Americans—the family represents a veritable cornerstone of civilization and any criticism of it is perceived as a radical anarchist attack on the essence of society itself. Understandably, feminists of the Victorian age concentrated on the single issue of suffrage to the exclusion of all others, but in the process they doomed themselves to eventual failure in terms of securing sexual equality.

By 1920 the suffragists had won the vote by securing the passage of the Nineteenth Amendment which enfranchised 26 million women of voting age. But legal facts do not necessarily coincide with political realities, and once again the historical process had a differential impact on the sexes, albeit the Nineteenth Amendment's impact is discernable both *within* the sexes as well as *between* them. Although we must avoid the error of assuming that the characteristics of men are the characteristics of the American people we must be equally cautious in assuming that the gains of white, middle-class women are the gains of working-class or black women.

Feminist leaders of the women's suffrage movement, like their male counterparts in the Progressive movement, were pre-eminently nativist, racist, and almost oblivious to the plight of the working-class or black American, male or female. Not only had such feminist leaders as Elizabeth Stanton and Susan Anthony referred derogatorily to the black man as "Sambo" in their campaign to defeat black male enfranchisement by the Fourteenth Amendment but suffragists in the South had even utilized the argument that female enfranchisement would help to preserve white supremacy in that region. Thus the net effect of the Nineteenth Amendment was to enfranchise white women legally in the United States and to deliver black women and men into the hands of the white supremacists in the South.[15]

The twenties are frequently cited as the decade of women's political and social emancipation in which "the New Woman" emerged as far as the manners and morals of America were concerned.[16]

> The flapper, as the "new woman" was called, was a creature of the 1920s. She smoked, drank, worked, and played side by side with men. She became preoccupied with sex—shocking and simultaneously unshockable. She danced close, became freer with her favors, kept her own latchkey, wore scantier attire which emphasized her boyish, athletic form, just as she used makeup and bobbed and dyed her hair.[17]

This "new woman" and new freedom, described in so many histories,[18] was largely the product of the city and these appellations applied only to those in the middle-income brackets who were white and free from household chores and yearly pregnancies via consumer and biological technology. The unparalleled freedom of the urban, white, middle-class woman hardly appertained to those who were poor, black, or lived in the country or smaller towns. Nonetheless, the appearance of the "new woman" in the city was a harbinger of the future and marked the rise of a mass-production-consumption economy in a country that was experiencing both rapid urbanization and expansion of its middle class. In the new urban family constellation, in which there were no more Indians to fight or log cabins to build and in which housework was becoming mechanized, the bond of marriage gradually began to shift from one of functional economics to one of affection. "We used to love each other because we needed each other. Now it is turned around. We need each other because we love each other. So the bonds are no longer functional, but affectional."[19]

Following the political and social gains of the white, middle-class urban woman during the twenties, many assumed that "the woman question" had been laid to rest and that the gates of entry into the man's world had been opened. Feminist ferment abated, and during the thirties and forties, when home life was threatened by the exigencies of the Great Depression and World War II, women generally emphasized the home and hearth, even while "Rosie the Riveter" was pulling up the slack in America's labor-hungry war industries.

Anxious to rebuild their families after the war, women gave up their jobs to the returning veterans, and much of white middle-class America moved from the cities to the suburbs, where for almost a generation the suburban woman experienced a new period of romanticized domesticity in which her identity was submerged into the world of her spouse and house and status was achieved by a new conformity by conspicuous consumption.

At the same time poor, rural black families, uprooted from their Southern moorings by a declining cotton economy and displaced by industrialization, made their way into the nation's ghettos. Lacking urban skills and suffering from racial discrimination at the hands of both labor and business, black men found themselves chronically unemployed and underemployed. The net result was that black wives, who had to go to work, had an easier time finding employment because domestic jobs were almost always available.[20] This reversal of roles, which almost invariably poisoned their marital relationships, resulted in "disrupted-marriages," male desertion, and female welfare.[21] Thus in 1963 while Betty Friedan was publishing her celebrated book, *The Feminine Mystique,* which denounced the boredom and restrictiveness of suburban affluence, her black counterparts in the urban ghettos were fighting a boredom of another sort—a boredom born of poverty, nurtured by a despairing apathy, and structured by broken male ambition.[22]

The New Feminists and the Contraceptive Culture

Betty Friedan's words fell mainly on the ears of the young women born of the generation of World War II—a generation which, like their feminist forebears a half-century earlier, was white, middle-class, and well-educated. Unlike any generation before them, however, it was the first to be raised entirely in a contraceptive age in which birth control methods offered women unprecedented sexual freedom.

Ms. Friedan's book, coming at a time when the black civil rights movement was at its height, produced a general concern among all other types of second-class citizens. Many of the women who

participated in the civil rights and student movements of the 1960s
found to their dismay that they even had to take a back seat to
the men of the New Left—cooking, typing, cleaning, and providing
occasional sex—while the men did all of the planning and confronting.
Stokely Carmichael summed up the female position in the movement
aptly, if crudely, when he said: "The only position for a woman
in SNCC [Student Non-Violent Coordinating Committee] is prone." [23]

Frustrated by sexist discrimination in the civil rights and student
movements, disillusioned with the war in Viet Nam, and spurred
by Betty Friedan's exposé of the vacuity of the suburban woman's
existence, women activists experienced a new self-awareness which
helped to launch the Women's Liberation Movement in 1966 when
Betty Friedan founded the National Organization for Women (NOW).
Using traditional civil rights tactics for winning legal and economic
rights for women, NOW is essentially a modern version of the old
feminist movement, which appeals to the same middle-class constituency and is dedicated to the reform rather than to a radical transformation of the institutions of American society.

Still the largest and most influential of the proliferating independent Women's Liberation groups,[24] its members have embraced the
nineteenth-century ideology of the oppression of women and equal
rights and have maintained its conviction "that what is good for
middle-class women is good for all women." [25] As a result, NOW's
reformist platform includes "equal pay and equal opportunities, paid
maternity leaves with guarantees for women to return to their jobs,
well-staffed and sound child-care centers in the communities or at
the places of employment, elimination of abortion laws, pensions
and severance pay for housewives, and an end to all discriminatory
practices both on the job and in public accommodations, to be
ensured, preferably, by the enactment of the Equal Rights Amendment." [26]

Coalescing with other reformist groups, NOW has been instrumental in pushing through Congress a bill that would ensure federal
support of a comprehensive system of child-care centers throughout
the nation at an initial cost of $2.1 billion. Although President Nixon
vetoed the bill in 1971, it appears certain that because women
constitute no less than 53.3 percent of the eligible voters in the
country it will remain a very lively issue.[27] NOW has also played

an important role in obtaining strict enforcement of the Civil Rights Act of 1964. In that act, partly as a joke and partly as a strategy to kill the bill, Representative Howard W. Smith of Virginia added "sex" to the standard list of race, color, religion, or national origin for which no one could be denied a job. With some laughter, Congress passed it, but women had the last laugh, for some 7500 of the 44,000 complaints filed through 1970 with the Equal Employment Opportunity Commission created by that law involved discrimination against women and have resulted in female jockeys, airline stewardesses who may work beyond the retirement age of 32, desegregated help-wanted ads in *The New York Times,* and suspended federal funds for universities involved in sex discrimination in job recruitment and assignments.[28]

Perhaps the most dramatic success of the reformist groups like NOW has been the resurrection of a 1923 constitutional amendment—the Equal Rights Amendment—which provides that equality of rights under the law shall not be denied or abridged by the United States or any state on account of sex. Approved by the Senate in March 1972, an election year, over Senator Sam Ervin's (D-North Carolina) protestations that passage would send women "into combat where they will be slaughtered," it will become the Twenty-Seventh Amendment to the Constitution if approved by three quarters of the states.[29]

Although NOW has maintained its middle-class reformist moorings, it has attempted to avoid the pitfalls of the past and has vainly striven to avoid rupturing the unity of the feminist movement by purging from its ranks the radicals and the separatists. This has been futile because NOW is not only too middle-class and middle-aged for many of the more radical women who were weaned on the revolutionary protest movements of the 1960s but its emphasis on job opportunities is basically counterproductive in terms of recruiting the poor and the black.

As new technology drastically reduces unskilled, semiskilled, and middle-management white collar jobs—some estimate at a rate of 40,000 a week or 2 million a year[30]—the workingmen and women, who under the present system have immense family responsibilities, will find an economic squeeze at the bottom which may pave the way for a bloody confrontation between middle-class women and the poor and blacks; and to win their demands for greater freedom and dignity in American society the women of the white middle class *must* have the poor and the minorities on their side. As Germaine Greer, author of *The Female Eunuch* has put it,

> . . . we must be part of the general pressure for revolution in a capitalist society. We can't be yet another privileged group applying pressure for our personal interests.[31]

No doubt this fact has contributed to the lack of success that middle-class reformist organizations like NOW have had in attracting the poor and the minorities into their ranks and accounts for the proliferation of radical women's groups across the country. To this, however, must be added the stimulus given to female radicalism by America's exploding technology of human reproduction which has now made it possible for women to challenge the probity of our commercial society, as well as question the validity of *the* basic American institution, the nuclear family.

With the development of such birth-control techniques as oral contraceptives and intrauterine loops, which may be left in the uterus indefinitely, women can now enjoy sex without the embarrassment of the famous diaphragm-fitting scene in Mary McCarthy's *The Group* and free themselves from the thrall of unwanted pregnancy. Moreover, the advent of artificial insemination and semen banks in which ovum and sperm can be stored even offers women the prospect of replicating human life without the necessity (or benefit) of sexual intercourse. All of this has not only emancipated women from the burden of childbearing and rearing but has also freed them from men.[32]

Faced with the injustices of second-class treatment in both marriage and the marketplace at a time when biological and industrial technology is reducing the necessity of female dependence on men to the junkheap of history, some of the radicals in the WLM (i.e., New York's new feminists and lesbians) have advocated a complete withdrawal from dependence on men, including sexual ties.

Most of the radicals, however, have adopted an ideological stance similar to that of the Redstockings; that is, blending the Marxian concept of class oppression with the rhetoric and tactics of the Black

Power movement to insist on the elimination of capitalism in favor of socialism and to discard the patriarchal nuclear family in favor of some sort of communal or extended family life in which childrearing would be shared and research on extrauterine reproduction accelerated.[33]

It is too bad that encounter groups like WITCH (Women's International Terrorists Conspiracy from Hell) and SCUM (Society for Cutting Up Men) have captured so much of the headlines with their Weathermen tactics and guerrilla theater antics,[34] for only by taking radical women seriously may we begin to assess the shortcomings of American society and make decisions about its future.

Conclusion

There is little value in weighing the ideologies of the radicals to determine whether their concepts of class oppression or the analogies they draw between blacks and women are an oversimplification. No doubt, like all ideologies, the radical ideologies are too simplistic, for all women are not oppressed in the same way, nor is their low status maintained by violence as is that of the black population.

More important than ideology—which is merely a device used by all interest groups to gain social leverage—is an appreciation of the fact that women are now functionally independent of having their destinies mapped out by men or heredity because of the liberating force of biological and industrial technology. Yet an archaic economic and familial structure in American society precludes this new-found freedom and equality from being converted into reality.

One thing is clear. The sexual division of labor in which the man acts as the head of family and breadwinner and the wife as homemaker no longer obtains. Spurred by the growing feminist rebellion, improved technology, and new sexual standards, the massive entrance of white women into full participation in American life may be only a generation away.[35]

How this entry will be breached remains a matter of conjecture. If it is done at the expense of the poor and black population—men and women—as it so often has in the past, no doubt it will be counterproductive and will exacerbate class and racial tensions even more than at present.

Women are now in a position to change the nature of a faulty society with the careful use of their new emancipation to gain for themselves the freedom and dignity that all human beings deserve. To do so the liberationists will have to avoid the mistakes of the past in which their actions had a differential impact on different classes and ethnic groups. This not only undermined the democratic character of their cause but it also reduced their effectiveness as a movement. If the goals of the Women's Liberation Movement can be meshed with those of the poor and ethnic minorities, the result may well be the liberation of men as well as women from the stultifying roles imposed on them by an agrarian past.

Notes

1. Ruth Rosen, "Sexism in History or, Writing Women's History Is a Tricky Business," *Journal of Marriage and the Family* (August 1971), 541–544.

2. Quoted in Egon Friedell, *A Cultural History of the Modern Age*, 3 vols. (New York, 1932), III, p. 7.

3. Samuel Eliot Morison, *The Oxford History of the American People* (New York: Oxford University Press, 1965), pp. 899–901. See the prefatory comments by Eleanor Flexner, *Century of Struggle* (New York: Atheneum, 1970), p. vii.

4. Henry Steele Commager, *The American Mind* (New Haven: Yale University Press, 1950), p. 424.

5. "Rebelling women—The Reason," *U.S. News and World Report* (April 13, 1970), 35; U.S. Department of Commerce, Bureau of the Census, "Poverty in the United States, 1959 to 1968," *Current Population Reports,* Series P-60, No. 68 (December 31, 1969), 2; reported in Kirsten Amundsen, *The Silenced Majority* (Englewood Cliffs: Prentice-Hall, 1971), pp. 29–30, 32, 94–95.

6. Page Smith, *Daughters of a Promised Land* (Boston: Little, Brown, 1970). Rosen, "Sexism in History," 542.

7. Rosen, "Sexism in History," 542.

8. David M. Potter, "American Women and the American Character," *Stetson University Bulletin,* LXII (January 1962), 1–22.

9. In a typical passage Turner concludes that, "These free lands promoted individualism, economic equality, freedom to rise, democracy." Frederick Jackson Turner, *The Frontier in American History* (New York: Holt, Rinehart and Winston, 1967), p. 259. Even female historians have overlooked the differential impact of history on women. Eleanor Flexnor, for example, concludes that the "frontier economy established a certain rough egali-

tarianism." *Century of Struggle*, p. 9. Professor Mary Lynn of Skidmore College correctly cautions that although the differential impact of the frontier on the sexes has been overlooked too much must not be made of it. "As early as the 17th century, colonial courts made important changes in the legal status of women in response to the frontier situation. Women gained some measure of control over inherited property, were permitted to enter into prenuptial contracts to protect the property they brought to a marriage, in some instances were allowed to sue or be sued, could exercise power of attorney, etc.—all expansions of the rights permitted English women under common law."

10. Edward A. Ross, *The Social Trend* (New York: The Century Co., 1922), p. 78–80. Sex alone, of course, did not determine the status of women in frontier settlements. Women also shared the status of men in their families, and if the men occupied a privileged position in society some of that privilege derogated to the women as well. Ross's distinction, however, is a bit overdrawn. In agrarian America women were frequently involved in the production of kitchen gardens, poultry, and dairy products. See Lydia Maria Child, *The American Frugal Housewife* (1833). Professor Georgia Carter has presciently observed that the manipulative role of women in the familial structure needs assessment before drawing any final conclusions regarding the status of women in America.

11. Quoted by Potter in "American Women and the American Character," p. 4,

12. Elizabeth Faulkner Baker, *Technology and Woman's Work* (New York: Columbia University Press, 1964), p. 9.

13. Edith Abbott, *Women in Industry: A Study in American Economic History* (New York: Appleton, 1910), pp. 53–54; Baker, *Technology and Woman's Work*, p. 9.

14. Gerda Lerner, "The Feminists: A Second Look," *Columbia Forum* (Fall 1970), p. 27; see also Gerda Lerner, "The Lady and the Mill Girl," *Midcontinent American Studies Journal*, X (Spring 1969), 5–15. I am indebted to the wisdom of Professor Mary Lynn in this area of the history of women.

15. Flexner, *Century of Struggle*, pp. 143–147; Warren Hinckle and Marianne Hinckle, "A History of the Rise of the Unusual Movement for Women Power in the United States 1961–1968," *Ramparts Magazine* (February 1968), 26.

16. Henry F. May, "Shifting Perspectives on the 1920's," *Mississippi Valley Historical Review*, **XLII** (December 1956), 405–427.

17. James R. McGovern, "The American Woman's Pre-World War I Freedom in Manners and Morals," *Journal of American History* (September 1968), 317.

18. See, for example, George E. Mowry, *The Urban Nation;* Frederick Lewis Allen, *Only Yesterday,* and Henry F. May, *The End of American Innocence.*

19. Flora Rheta Schreiber and Melvin Herman, "Battle of the Sexes," *Science Digest* (April 1967), 23.

20. Charles E. Silberman, *Crisis in Black and White* (New York: Vintage, 1964), p. 118.

21. Jessie Bernard, *Marriage And Family Among Negroes* (Englewood Cliffs, New Jersey: Prentice-Hall, 1966), pp. 101–103; Dr. Bernard defines a "disrupted marriage" as a family broken by either divorce or separation.

22. Speaking of apathy and boredom as an ancient form of protest against oppression, Saul Alinsky has observed that in the ghetto it represents a refusal on the part of the black man to cooperate with his oppressor. As he puts it, "You can force a man to live in prison, but you can't make him contribute to its upkeep." Quoted in Silberman, *Black and White,* p. 48.

23. Presumably, Carmichael means supine.

24. *Time* magazine estimates that NOW's 1972 membership is close to 18,000 and has about 255 chapters in 48 states. "Women's Liberation Revisited," *Time* (March 20, 1972), 29.

25. Lerner, "The Feminists," p. 26; "Who's Come a Long Way, Baby?", *Time* (August 31, 1970), 16–21.

26. Amundsen, *The Silenced Majority,* p. 160. There is far more *pluribus* than *unum* within NOW as in the Women's Liberation Movement as a whole. Because there is no centralized authority in any of the organizations and women have worked conscientiously to avoid the "cult of the personality," the agenda of NOW or any other organization should be taken as a representative rather than a definitive list.

27. *Congressional Record,* July 10, 1970, p. 1745.

28. Morton Hunt, "Up Against The Wall, Male Chauvinist Pig!," *Playboy* (May 1970), 102; Joreen, "The 51 Percent Minority Group: A Statistical Essay," in *Sisterhood is Powerful* (New York: Vintage, 1970), pp. 37–46; John Stowell, "Feminists Hit at Sex Bias on 300 Campuses," *Los Angeles Times,* December 15, 1971, 5.

29. Hawaii, Nebraska, New Hampshire, Delaware, Iowa, and Idaho ratified the amendment within a few days; California rejected it.

30. See Ben Seligman, *Most Notorious Victory* (New York: Free Press, 1966).

31. "Playboy Interview: GERMAINE GREER," *Playboy* (January 1972), 64.

32. Shulamith Firestone, in *The Dialectic of Sex,* argues that biology is inherently oppressive but that biological technology and abortion hold the promise of delivering women from their primary oppression. Biological science or not, sexual differences continue to produce legal discrimination against women. By way of example, only 22 states in the Union have laws that subject clients of prostitution to penalty, though all 50 place penalties on the female vendor. See Charles Winick and Paul K. Kinsie, *The Lively Commerce: Prostitution in the United States* (New York: Signet, 1971), pp. 208–209.

33. Margaret B. McDowell, "The New Rhetoric of Woman Power," *The Midwest Quarterly* (January 1971), 189.

34. Guerrilla theater groups have burned bras, wigs, and Barbie dolls and on stage have portrayed women with huge, grotesque breasts who screamed lines at those who took the parts of their male oppressors. Female "libbers" at the University of Illinois attacked one male student, tore open his shirt, pulled down his pants, and threatened to rape him. WITCH gains attention by releasing hundreds of white mice at weddings and chanting hexes on Wall Street.

35. Zbigniew Brzezinski, *Between Two Ages: America's Role in the Technetronic Era* (New York: Viking, 1970), p. 270; like so many authors, Professor Brzezinski shows little concern for class or ethnicity when it comes to a discussion of women in America.

FROM SIX . . .

Throughout American history women's rights have made the most headway during times of national ferment or crisis, such as the Civil War and World War I. Interposed between these two conflagrations was the severe economic depression of the 1890's and the Populist crusade which drew its sustenance from those hard times. Significantly, a number of women, which included Mary Elizabeth Lease, Annie Diggs, Sarah Emery, and Eva McDonald Valesh, played prominent roles in the Populist movement, which rather cautiously sponsored women's suffrage. Ultimately, however, Populism was directed against an inequitable corporate system that benefited only a few at the expense of the many. Although the old People's Party lapsed into oblivion after the Presidential election of 1908, the spirit of Populism is revisiting the American political scene today.

. . . ON TO SEVEN

We meet in the midst of a nation brought to the verge of moral, political and material ruin. . . . The people are demoralized. . . . The newspapers are largely subsidized, public opinion silenced . . . , homes covered with mortgages, labor impoverished, and the land concentrating in the hands of capitalists. . . . The fruits of the toil of millions are boldly stolen to build up colossal fortunes for a few.

Populist Party platform, 1892

SEVEN

FROM HAYSEEDS TO HARD-HATS: AMERICAN POPULISM REVISITED

THOMAS J. OSBORNE

"Populism is undergoing a revival," declared a recent *Time* magazine editorial.[1] During the last several years a spate of books and articles on the New Populism have made their appearance. Not since the McCarthy purges of the early 1950s has so much attention been focused on the recurrent Populist theme in American politics. The angry voices of middle Americans make up the resounding chorus of protest that now echoes across the land. Ignored during the 1960s by politicians who seemed preoccupied with campus and ghetto unrest, these hard-working, tax-paying, blue-collar stalwarts are no longer content to remain the unsung heroes of the "silent majority." Instead, the urban white workingmen of today, like their rural agrarian counterparts of the 1890s, have decided to enter the political arena and vocalize their grievances.

Discontent abounds in the laboring class. Blue-collar workers who support moderate-sized families on incomes averaging $10,700 a year are scarcely able to meet expenses in the face of rising prices and taxes, yet welfare recipients living in working-class neighborhoods do not have to scramble for job overtime nor are they expected to help shoulder an increasing tax burden. In anger and disgust the "little man" has watched unemployed college students and ethnic minorities parade through the streets of the nation's capital carrying placards that demanded recognition of "welfare rights."

At the upper end of the financial spectrum are the highly educated professional and managerial types that constitute what John Kenneth Galbraith terms the New Class. According to federal government statistics, people in this category, i.e., those whose families earn in excess of $15,000 per year, paid only 28 percent of their income in taxes in 1968, whereas families in lower income brackets paid 33 percent.[2] The tax burden of the lower middle class waxes even more inequitably when we consider that in 1968 there were 21 people with incomes of more than 1 million dollars who paid no taxes whatsoever. In addition, 381 people with incomes in excess of $500,000 were exempt from taxation.

Sandwiched between the exploiters from above and below, the average American workingman has grown weary of the squeeze. Having contributed more than his fair share of the blood and treasure expended in Vietnam while seeing his patriotism mocked by panhandling students attending publicly financed universities that seldom graduate his own children (but offer lucrative scholarships to ungrateful ethnic minorities and afford sanctuary to lawbreaking militants), America's blue-collar workers refuse to tread water psychically or financially any longer. Their deep sense of alienation, insecurity, betrayal, and indignation makes them vulnerable to unscrupulous politicians and demagogues who provide them with facile scapegoats and panaceas in return for their electoral support at the polls.

The direction that this new urban Populist movement will take seems uncertain. Much will depend, of course, on the health of the national economy, the extent of America's overseas involvement, and the resourcefulness with which our leaders combat the domestic problems of racism, crime, poverty, and pollution. By carefully examining the Populism of the 1890's, however, perhaps we can gain some historically comparable insight into the pitfalls and possibilities of its modern variant.

Before the two Populist movements can be compared, it is necessary to point out that few historians acknowledge any significant connection between the old and new Populism. The view of Yale Professor C. Vann Woodward seems to reflect the consensus among historians that whatever similarities appear to exist they are far outweighed by the differences.[3] Woodward argues that the Populist movement of the 1890s was spawned in the middle of a severe economic depression, that the problems these rural discontents encountered were largely agricultural, and that, unlike today's fragmented movement, the old Populists were organized politically into a third party. Furthermore, Woodward claims that the parochial outlook and evangelical style of the old Populism are not characteristic of its present-day counterpart. Although these differences are not to be taken lightly, it will be shown that the two political movements have much in common.

Nineteenth-century Populism was basically a rural agrarian reform movement spearheaded by small southern and midwestern farmers who were plagued by rising overhead costs, declining grain prices, and underrepresentation in the national government. Eastern capitalists invariably topped the farmers' list of public offenders. "Wall Street owns the country," inveighed Mary Elizabeth Lease, who exhorted her listeners to "raise less corn and more hell."[4] What followed was a veritable pentecost of politics that culminated in William Jennings Bryan's defeat in the election of 1896. Populism rapidly declined after that, but many of the party's proposals were eventually enacted into law.[5] Although historians seem to be in basic accord on the composition and achievements of the Populists, an acrimonious debate on the nature and ultimate goals of the late nineteenth-century reform movement[6] continues to divide scholars.

Richard Hofstadter, one of the foremost historians of Populism, perceptively recognized its dual nature—its pragmatic and reasonable "hard" side and its romantic and irrational "soft" side. In his Pulitzer

Prize-winning study *The Age of Reform* (1955) Hofstadter readily acknowledged that "in their concrete programs . . . they added most constructively to our political life."[7] There was also a "soft" side to agrarian radicalism that derived from its larger world view. The dominant characteristics of this flaccid underside include the idealization of the common man, the myth of a past golden age, the concept of natural harmonies, the dualistic view of social conflicts, the conspiracy theory of history, xenophobic nationalism, and the strong visceral inclination to support "wars for humanity."

Perhaps the fundamental article of faith in the Populist creed was an abounding belief in the innate goodness of mankind. In *The Golden Bottle,* a political novel written by Ignatius Donnelly, the eloquent "sage of Nininger" extolled this natural goodness:

> Man is the only thing worth considering in this great world. He is the climax of the creative force; the ultimate object for which this planet was made; a *little god* working out the purposes of the Great God.[8]

The Populists surely did not originate the cult of the common man, but few social movements in American history have manifested a higher regard for ordinary people than these hopeful nineteenth-century reformers.

Man's inherent virtues were nourished or blighted, as the case may be, by his environment. For the Populists there was no setting more conducive to man's happiness than the mythical agrarian Eden of early nineteenth-century America. Thomas E. Watson, the irascible Populist Governor of Georgia, wistfully asserted that "during the first half-century of our national existence, we had no poor."[9] If many Populists looked back on the halcyon years of the yeoman republic with nostalgia and affection, they seemed to harbor forebodings and disdain for the new age of industrialism and commercial farming. "Formerly the tools of agriculture were the wagon and the plow," observed the prominent Kansas Supreme Court Justice, Frank Doster. "Now," he lamented, "the terrible elements of physical nature—steam, electricity, [and] compressed air—are utilized to do the work of man."[10]

In the legendary arcadia about which Populists fondly reminisced, there existed a near-perfect harmony of interests. Unwittingly they rejected James Madison's notion of multiple and competing economic factions. The People's Party pretended to be everything that its appellation implied, namely, the vigorous and undaunted spokesman for all downtrodden groups. Party leaders failed or refused to recognize, for example, that farmers and laborers oftentimes had conflicting material interests.[11]

The only societal division that seemed to concern these agrarian reformers was the proverbial class struggle between labor and capital. "There are but two sides in the conflict that is being waged in this country today," declared a Populist manifesto, and they were clearly delineated:

> On the one side are the allied hosts of monopolies, the money power, great trusts and railroad corporations. . . . On the other are the farmers, laborers, merchants, and all other people who produce wealth and bear the burdens of taxation.[12]

As the above quotation suggests, Populist rhetoric tended to ignore intraclass economic differences while discounting fundamental ethnocultural particularities. Dichotomizing in this fashion was not without its advantages, however. In addition to simplifying the nature of social conflicts, it promoted a semblance of unity among divergent interest groups and depicted the plutocratic enemy as a highly visible monolith.

For a variety of understandable reasons Populists were addicted to conspiracy theories. The nefarious activities of Jay Gould and James Fisk coupled with the odious machinations of Credit Mobilier, the Whiskey Ring, and the reprehensible carpetbag regimes in the South—all of these unsavory episodes predisposed angry debtridden farmers to view post-Civil War American history as a colossal conspiracy perpetrated by the money power. "The farmer has been the victim of a gigantic scheme of spoliation," exclaimed Kansas Senator William A. Peffer.[13] At times this web of subterfuge assumed global proportions, as the "Omaha Platform" of the People's Party bluntly testified:

> A vast conspiracy against mankind has been organized on two continents, and it is rapidly taking possession of the

world. If not met and overthrown at once, it forbodes terrible
social convulsions, the destruction of civilization, or the establishment of an absolute despotism.[14]

Among some of the more paranoid members of the Party, these
conspiratorial fantasies conjured up virulent strains of anti-Semitism
and nativism, although it should be added that these maledictions
were seldom translated into pogroms against Jews or other ethnic
minorities. Rhetorical anti-Semitism, nevertheless, was a standard
theme in Populist literature, especially in the political novels of Coin
Harvey and Ignatius Donnelly. "The aristocracy of the world is now
almost altogether of Hebrew origin," warned one of Donnelly's
fictional characters.[15] These wealthy Jewish businessmen, especially
the financiers, were caricatured as gouging Shylocks who constituted
the international gold ring led by Baron James Rothschild.[16]

Coupled with Populist anti-Semitism was a profound contempt
for immigrants and, at times, Negroes. In describing some of the
recent arrivals from eastern Europe, Thomas E. Watson exhorted
that "the scum of creation has been dumped on us. Some of our
principal cities are more foreign than American."[17] The strident
Anglo-Saxonism of Mary Lease probably went far beyond the eco-
nomically inspired nativism of many Populists, but the racial bigotry
displayed by this prominent Midwesterner indicates that discriminatory attitudes were not restricted to the southern wing of the People's
Party. According to Mrs. Lease, Caucasians should take over the
tropics in both hemispheres and enslave Negroes and Orientals.
"Through all the vicissitudes of time, the Caucasian has arisen to
the moral and intellectual supremacy of the world," she affirmed.
"Now this favored race is fitted for the stewardship of the earth
and emancipation from manual labor."[18]

When the People's Party was organized in 1891, it solicited support
from southern Negro farmers who were subject to the same economic
and political disadvantages as their white counterparts. This part-
nership was short-lived. Bryan's defeat in 1896, coupled with the
charge by southern Democrats that their third-party brethren were
pro-Negro, caused some southern Populists to look for a scapegoat.
As Populism turned from reform to reaction, the southern "middle-
of-the-roaders" resorted to the verbal and physical harassment of
Negroes. One influential Populist supporter of Alabama Governor

Reuben F. Kolb publicly denounced Negro voting and favored "shooting evey God damned one who goes to the polls to cast his ballot!"[19] As the turbulent decade of the nineties drew to a close, Thomas Watson, the twice-nominated Populist vice-presidential candidate, became an ardent spokesman for white supremacy. "What does civilization owe to the Negro?" mused Watson. "Nothing! *Nothing! ! NOTHING! ! !*" he retorted.[20]

In harmony with the xenophobic nationalism of some party extremists was a strong visceral tendency to support "wars for humanity" in general and the Spanish-American War in particular. After having been soundly defeated by the eastern business interests in 1896, the tattered and angry farmers shifted their priority of demands from "free silver to free Cuba." Armed with the same righteous indignation that carried them into earlier battles, Populists attacked Wall Street capitalists for their callous indifference toward the inhumane debaucheries committed by Spanish officials in Cuba. Although jingoism in 1898 was not confined to any class, section, or party, the flood of popular support for this needless war came largely from the same rural areas in which Populism was firmly rooted.[21]

Having examined the dark side of the late nineteenth century Populism, we can now match its silhouette against the shadowy profile of its modern counterpart. Naturally, the urban-industrial setting for the new movement, its loose political organization, and aversion to socialism distinguish it from its predecessor of the 1890s. These major differences notwithstanding, the retrograde features of traditional Populism are highly visible on the American political landscape today.

Eric Hoffer, the renowned longshoreman and wry commentator on American life, celebrated the innate goodness of disadvantaged people in *The Ordeal of Change* (1963). After surveying the numerous contributions of "common folk" and "undesirables," he concluded:

> Small wonder that we in this country have a deeply ingrained faith in human regeneration. We believe that, given a chance, even the degraded and the apparently worthless are capable of constructive work and great deeds.[22]

Significantly, this optimism was not expressed by a sheltered academician whose acquaintance with mankind was acquired in vicarious

reading of Jefferson or Emerson. Instead, this estimate was made
by a seasoned America watcher who spent a generation working
and reflecting on the San Francisco waterfront. The reference to
"we" in the above quotation suggests that many of the men who
work with Hoffer share this benign outlook.

"Those Were the Days" is the theme song for CBS's Emmy Award
winning program "All in the Family" which features the sardonic
wit of Archie Bunker, America's favorite hard-hat (a modern counterpart of Finley Peter Dunne's Mr. Hennessy). Each serialized showing
of this weekly televised program is prefaced with a rendition of
this musical eulogy to early twentieth-century America when life
was uncomplicated by welfare poachers, radical feminists, and icono-
clastic hippies. This paean to the past is indicative of the older white
workingman's nostalgic affection for the good old days which is
reinforced by an equally strong aversion to the present. John Filiatreau, a journalist who writes for the Louisville *Courier-Journal*,
claims that this tendency to romanticize the past is especially true
of southern white laborers. "For most of the present century," writes
this labor-affairs specialist, "the worker of the South has remained
in a bygone time, jailed in a regional mythology so potent he continues to believe it."[23]

Today's Populists seem quite hopeful of putting together a new
political coalition comprised of working-class whites and blacks,
liberal intellectuals, and recently enfranchised young voters. Jack
Newfield and Jeff Greenfield, coauthors of *A Populist Manifesto:
The Making of a New Majority* (1972), optimistically argue that the
New Populism is a movement based on class rather than race or
culture.[24] In short, these writers are trumpeting the same "harmony
of interests" doctrine that deluded their nineteenth-century predecessors. The failure of a reform-minded Democratic Party to assemble
such a coalition in 1972 and the landslide election victory of Richard
Nixon should dispel any doubts about combining such heterogeneous
and combustible elements.

"It is us they is always chokin' so that the rich folks can stay
fat," complained a young white Kentucky coal miner to a reporter
from *The New York Times*.[25] "Us" and "they" represent for this and
a host of other discouraged blue-collar workers the division of society
into two hostile camps—the affluent managers and professionals of

the New Class and the disadvantaged "working stiffs" of the producing class. This simple dualistic view of social conflict provides a
semblance of unity among factious laborers and makes it easier for
them to identify the enemy.

For some new Populists "the enemy" constitutes a ring of international financiers, including Wall Street brokers, who steer the American ship of state through troughs of depression and over crests of
prosperity toward involvement in profitable overseas wars. "Most
of the wars to which America has been a party throughout our history
. . . , not excepting Vietnam," states the 1972 American Party
platform, "have resulted from the machinations of international
finance in their centuries-old drive toward world government." [26]
This devil's theory of history, which is reminiscent of pronouncements
contained in the Omaha Platform of 1892, is advanced by the party
which claims to speak for "the majority of Americans [who are]
hard-working, productive, tax-paying citizens." [27]

Although any hint of overt anti-Semitism has been scrupulously
averted by American Party leaders, some rather veiled strains of
this age-old prejudice can be detected within the party's ranks.
Several of George Wallace's 1968 campaign strategists had notorious
reputations for harboring anti-Semitic conspiratorial views.[28] Also,
some leading American Party figures have openly endorsed *None
Dare Call It Conspiracy* by Gary Allen, a book which reads like
some of the more polemical Populist tracts of the 1890s. After linking
the Bolshevik Revolution of 1917 to a cartel of international bankers,
Allen attempts to clinch his argument by stating that "for over 150
years it has been standard operating procedure of the Rothschild's
and their allies [Allen mentions Kuhn-Loeb, Lazard Frères, Lehman
Bros., Goldman-Sachs, et al.] to control both sides of every conflict." [29] It is interesting to note that a recent study by Gertrude
J. Selznick and Stephen Steinberg indicates that resentment of Jews
is much more prevalent among blue-collar workers (who have given
the American Party enthusiastic support) than among any other
salaried group.[30]

Aside from its latent but mild anti-Semitic tendencies, the American Party is known for exhibiting other nativistic impulses. The
immigration plank in their 1972 platform is similar to the stand
taken by the old Populists:

The mass importation of peoples with low standards of living
threatens the wage structure of the American working man
and, frequently, the political subversion of our American
institutions.[31]

As a corrective the party proposes that immigration be restricted
to persons originating from Western European countries or to "other
people who share our general cultural traditions and background."[32]
Although Wallace rarely delivers speeches that are as explicitly racist
as his 1962 "segregation forever" address, his views on busing
and school integration are applauded by many of his working-class
supporters.

In June 1971 a rumor spread through Rosedale, Queens—a blue-
collar suburb of New York City made up of Irish, Jews, and Ital-
ians—that a black man had bought a house in the neighborhood
and planned to move in with his white wife and a dozen other
relatives. The reaction of the residents to this unfounded gossip
poignantly reveals the traditional Negrophobia that grips numerous
white workingmen. With axes and picks they rampaged through the
unoccupied house, shattering windows, ripping out fixtures, destroying the plumbing, and scrawling grafitti on the walls: "We hate
niggers. . . . Stamp out niggers." Meanwhile a throng of some 200
onlookers gathered outside and cheered the deeds of this local demo-
lition squad.[33] As this grim incident shows, the problem of maintaining
harmonious race relations among working-class people seems, at
times, insurmountable. Even leftist intellectuals like Michael Harrington occasionally despair the fact that unions recruit so many
"young whites attracted by the populist racism of George Wallace."[34]

Just as the old People's Party tended to support American involvement in the Cuban imbroglio of the 1890s, likewise today's Populists
seem to condone America's intervention in Vietnam. Professor Ronald
Radosh has demonstrated that the AFL-CIO leadership subscribes
to the Cold War shibboleth that a monolithic Communist bloc
threatens to engulf "free nations."[35] In August 1966 the Executive
Board of the AFL-CIO met and issued a strong statement supporting
the buildup of U.S. forces in Vietnam. Any disruption of the war
effort, declared the Board,

can only pollute and poison the bloodstream of our democracy. . . . Those who would deny our military forces unstinting

support are, in effect, aiding the Communist enemy of our country.[36]

During the Cambodian intervention of 1970 George Meany, president of the AFL-CIO, publicly announced that he backed this new offensive. The propensity of organized labor to support the Vietnam War was also illustrated by the Wall Street demonstration of May 1970. Amid chants of "All the way U.S.A." and "Love it or leave it" a contingent of some 200 construction workers surged through Wall Street and beat up nearly 60 war protesters. This unseemly incident was followed by a mass demonstration of 100,000 workingmen who surrounded City Hall on May 20 to express their support of the war in Southeast Asia. Peter J. Brennan, who now serves as President Nixon's Secretary of Labor, praised the blue-collar stalwarts for their display of patriotism.[37]

It has been shown that the darker side of late nineteenth century Populism, call it the hayseed syndrome, has survived into the 1970s. The provincial-mindedness of the old agrarian reformers is matched by a similar myopia characteristic of the new hard-hat mentality. According to some political analysts, this retrograde tendency within Populism augurs a sweep of the political pendulum to the far right.

Political scientist Victor C. Ferkiss argues that fascism is an indigenous growth on the American body politic and that its roots are to be found in the Populist movement of the 1890s.[38] After alluding to most of the features adumbrated in the preceding pages of this chapter, Ferkiss concludes that the old Populists became impatient with the cumbersome nature of the democratic processes and opted not for liberalism but for direct, plebiscitary democracy. Thus the seeds of American fascism were sown in the late nineteenth century and sprouted into the folkish nostrums of Huey Long, Father Coughlin, and Gerald L. K. Smith.

The implications of this view for the future of American politics are profound. Kevin Phillips's shrewd analysis of the 1968 presidential election shows that a stable and conservative Republican majority of about 57 percent has emerged. It is comprised of Wallace voters, the "sun belt" cities of the South and Southwest, urban workingmen, and voters in "the Heartlands." Furthermore, Phillips states that this conservative coalition can maintain power without Negro votes.[39] The appeals of right-wing Populism to these sectors is an ominous sign of what may lie on the political horizon. Populism is, indeed, undergoing a revival; hopefully, our knowledge of its historic pitfalls can help us realize its salutary possibilities.

Notes

1. *Time* (April 17, 1972), 27.

2. Patricia Cayo Sexton and Brendan Sextan, *Blue Collars and Hard-Hats: The Working Class and the Future of American Politics* (New York: Vintage, 1971), p. 155.

3. The New York *Times* Magazine (June 4, 1972), 16–17, 60, 63–64, 66–69.

4. John D. Hicks, *The Populist Revolt: A History of the Farmers' Alliance and the People's Party* (Lincoln, Nebraska: University of Nebraska Press, 1961), p. 160.

5. *Ibid.*, pp. 404–423 contain a thorough discussion of Populist measures that Congress enacted into law during the Progressive Era.

6. For a good introduction to the literature on this controversy see Sheldon Hackney, Ed., *Populism: The Critical Issues* (Boston: Little, Brown, 1971).

7. Richard Hofstadter, *The Age of Reform: From Bryan to F.D.R.* (New York: Vintage, 1955), p. 61.

8. Norman Pollack, Ed., *The Populist Mind* (New York: Bobbs-Merrill, 1967), p. 494. Emphasis added.

9. Hofstadter, *Age of Reform*, p. 62. The existence of abject poverty in early America is demonstrated by Raymond A. Mohl in "Poverty in Early America: The Case of Eighteenth Century New York City," *New York History* (January, 1969), 5–27.

10. Pollack, *Populist Mind*, p. 12.

11. Ordinarily the farmer needs high-priced agricultural commodities, low-priced manufactured goods, and low wages. The laborer, however, needs low-priced farm products, high-priced manufactured wares, and high wages. See Norman J. Ware, *The Labor Movement in the United States: 1860–1895* (New York: Vintage, 1929), pp. 352–355.

12. Ray Allen Billington, *Westward Expansion: A History of the American Frontier*, 3d ed. (New York: Macmillan, 1967), p. 743.

13. Pollack, *Populist Mind*, p. 91.

14. *Ibid.*, p. 61.

15. Ignatius Donnelly, *The Golden Bottle* (New York, 1892), p. 280, cited by Hofstadter, *Age of Reform*, p. 79.

16. *Ibid.*, p. 78.

17. Thomas E. Watson, *The Life and Times of Andrew Jackson* (Thomson, Georgia, 1912), p. 326.

18. Mary E. Lease, *The Problem of Civilization Solved* (Chicago, 1895), p. 17.

19. Robert Saunders, "Southern Populists and the Negro, 1893–1895," *Journal of Negro History*, **LIV** (July 1969), 261; see also Charles Crowe, "Tom Watson, Populists, and Blacks Reconsidered," *Journal of Negro History*, **LV** (April 1970), 99–116.

20. C. Vann Woodward, *Tom Watson: Agrarian Rebel* (New York: Oxford University Press, 1969), p. 380.

21. Joseph E. Wisan, *The Cuban Crisis as Reflected in the New York Press, 1895–1898* (New York: Octagon, 1965), p. 455.

22. Eric Hoffer, *The Ordeal of Change* (New York: Harper & Row, 1963), p. 150.

23. John Filiatreau, "The White Worker in the South," *Dissent* (Winter, 1972), 78.

24. Jack Newfield and Jeff Greenfield, *A Populist Manifesto: The Making of a New Majority* (New York: Warner, 1972), p. 42.

25. *The New York Times*, September 24, 1972, p. 14; see also *The Christian Century* (May 7, 1969), 646; and *The New Republic* (January 22, 1972), 18–20.

26. The Platform of the American Party, Foreign Policy, Vietnam.

27. *Ibid.*, Preamble.

28. Seymour Martin Lipset and Earl Raab, *The Politics of Unreason: Right-Wing Extremism in America, 1790N1970* (New York: Harper & Row, 1970), pp. 351–355.

29. Gary Allen, *None Dare Call It Conspiracy* (Rossmore, California: Concord, 1972), pp. 75–75.

30. Gertrude J. Selznick and Stephen Steinberg, *The Tenacity of Prejudice: Anti-Semitism in Contemporary America* (New York: Harper & Row, 1969), pp. 74–75. Recent studies by Thomas F. Pettigrew and Robert T. Riley, Samuel Lubell, and Clark Kissinger attest to Wallace's strength among laborers in industrial cities.

31. The Platform of the American Party, Foreign Policy, Immigration.

32. *Ibid.*

33. *The New York Times*, June 12, 1972, p. 31.

34. Michael Harrington, *Old Working Class, New Working Class*," *Dissent* (Winter, 1972), 146.

35. Ronald Radosh, *American Labor and United States Foreign Policy: The Cold War in the Unions from Gompers to Lovestone* (New York: Random House, 1969), p. 446.

36. *Ibid.*, p. 444

37. *The Nation* (June 15, 1970), 716.

38. Victor C. Ferkiss, "Populist Influences on American Fascism," *Western Political Quarterly*, 'x:2 (June 1957), 350–357.

39. Kevin P. Phillips, *The Emerging Republican Majority* (New Rochelle, New York: Arlington House, 1969), p. 468.

FROM SEVEN . . .

Although the conservation of America's natural resources was not a salient feature of the Populist platform, concern for the environment was beginning to show in the 1890s with the passage of the Forest Reserve Act, the establishment of Yosemite National Park, and the founding of the Sierra Club. During the Progressive Era which followed a full-scale conservationist movement was launched by President Theodore Roosevelt. Although commercial and aesthetic considerations figured most prominently in the Progressive conservationist movement, a third factor, survival, has been the animating force behind today's ecology crusade. During both periods alarmed publicists and political leaders have focused needed attention on "Politics and the Environment."

. . . ON TO EIGHT

In the West our desire to conquer nature often means simply that we diminish the probability of small inconveniences at the cost of increasing the probability of very large disasters.

Kenneth Boulding
Human Values on the Spaceship Earth

EIGHT

POLITICS
AND THE ENVIRONMENT

FRED R. MABBUTT

The rise of the United States from infancy to maturity has been virtually synonymous with the rise of the modern Western world, for it has not only been the vanguard of constitutional government but of modern technology as well. Such an assertion may legitimately evoke curiosity regarding what is meant by the phrase "modern world." How does it differ from the premodern world? What are its characteristics?

Such a query may be answered by sketching the characteristics of the premodern world to set it apart from an age that is modern.

One may turn to any number of classical works, including the *Bible*, to find a statement that describes the human condition and provides a record of man's relation to nature. In *Genesis* 3, for example, we find that man has been cast out of Paradise (or what a political scientist would term utopia) into the world of reality. Its description of the human condition is worth recalling, not so much for its theological meaning as for its accuracy in describing premodern societies then and now.

> Cursed is the ground for thy sake; in sorrow shalt thou eat of it all the days of thy life; Thorns also and thistles shall it bring forth to thee; and thou shalt eat the herb of the field; In the sweat of thy face shalt thou eat bread, till thou return unto the ground; for out of it was thou taken: for dust thou art, and unto dust shalt thou return.

Thus the essence of the human condition in premodern societies is pain and penury, followed by early death. In other words, premodernity was and is characterized by the tyranny of nature over man and partly as a consequence the tyranny of man over man. A modern nation like the United States, by contrast, is a society in which man dominates and not infrequently tyrannizes nature and is cemented together by a constitutional government based on the principle of political equality.

Premodern man viewed nature's bounty as finite and *ipso facto* fatalistically accepted the moral necessity of curbing the human appetite and submitting to the tyranny of nature and the despotism of both secular and religious authorities. His wretched political and material existence was accepted as a trying prelude to the Spiritual Life hereafter.

Conversely, modern man has viewed nature's resources to be almost without limit and has been bent on bringing heaven to earth by destroying the curses of *Genesis*. The late President Lyndon Johnson did not invent the "War on Poverty"; it has been going on since the founding of our Republic. Like all modern men, we have reversed the historical process, and instead of allowing nature to tyrannize us we have tyrannized nature, torturing out of her her secrets and resources to make war on the apocolyptic horsemen of pain, penury, and death.

At the heart of the modern effort to alleviate man's historic human condition has been the philosophy of modern science as it is found in Sir Francis Bacon's *Novum Organum* rather than the premodern science of a Socrates as it is described in Aristophanes' *The Clouds.* Aristophanes tells us in *The Clouds* that premodern scientists like Socrates busied themselves with such experiments as measuring how far a flea could jump and determining whether a gnat hummed through its mouth or its rump. Such inquisitiveness provided knowledge for knowledge's sake, or what we today would term pure or theoretical science, but it did little to alleviate the tribulation of the human condition in a premodern age.

Sir Francis Bacon, one of the world's first modern scientists, likened these earlier scientists to little boys full of windy arguments but impotent in terms of improving man's human condition. He argued that man should *apply* his knowledge and create a technological science to help man escape the curse of *Genesis* and provide relief for man's estate. We must, he argued, torture out of nature its treasure and secrets so that we can dominate it. So successfully have modern scientists heeded Bacon's advice that they have replaced the priests as sources of authority and provided us with a counterpart to the Biblical pillars of fire by night with their thermonuclear explosions.

Only within the last decade has science as a source of authority come into question. Thus, although at the start of the twentieth century books like John Fiske's *The Life Everlasting* could confidently make assurances that science and technology would end only in man's increased freedom and material well-being, books at the end of the twentieth century like Rachael Carson's *The Silent Spring* were warning of ecological disaster because of man's misguided use of nature.

The publication of *The Silent Spring* in 1962 is commonly credited with touching off our present conservation or ecology movement.[1] More likely our innocent faith in the modern scientist came to an end, or at least was significantly tarnished, on a night in November 1965 when all electric power collapsed in an 80,000-square-mile area of the northeastern United States and Canada. As Barry Commoner described it, "The breakdown was a total surprise. For hours engineers and power officials were unable to turn the lights on again; for days no one could explain why they went out; even now no

one can promise that it won't happen again."[2] The effects of this
event not only shattered the myth of the omniscience of science
but served to highlight what many Americans already sensed: that
like the Sorcerer's Apprentice the blessings of modern science were
mixed and possibly out of hand, that the technological triumphs of
modern science had not only helped Americans defeat the cure of
Genesis and propel astronauts to the heavens but that these triumphs
were clouded by the pollution and destruction of our environment.

Though distracted by a nagging and angry war in Vietnam, thousands of university professors, students, and private citizens joined
hands in the mid-1960s to form new kinds of interest groups like
Common Cause and Friends of the Earth to challenge our national
priorities, obtain injunctions against the rape of mother nature, hold
environmental-teach-ins,[3] and generally lobby for legislation that
would not only preserve nature's bounty but would maintain an
ecological harmony between man and the rest of nature.

Such action was not without precedent in American history, for
America in the past had experienced two major conservation movements,[4] and some of the earlier conservation groups like the Sierra
Club were still alive and well and ready to take to the field to
do battle in America's third conservation movement.

The first of these conservation movements was preceded by a
spate of utopian experiments during the ante-bellum Civil War period
which ranged from Brook Farm to Thoreau's Walden Pond. These
experiments represented ecological ideas that, like Leonardo da
Vinci's technological discoveries in his premarket world, had come
to fruition before their time. The generation and growth of America's
first conservation movement was stimulated by the environment itself
as that area of free land on the western edge of our advancing
settlements known as the frontier came to an end. The Census Report
of 1890, which announced this fact, challenged the comfortable
American delusion that our natural resources were infinite.

With the political support of a "rough and ready" popular president, Theodore Roosevelt, who had lived in and loved the West,
and a core of scientists, bureaucrats, and congressmen dedicated to
infusing scientific rationality and "the gospel of efficiency"[5] into
the use of our natural resources, the first conservation movement
hit full stride during the first decade of the twentieth century.

By the time that Roosevelt became president in 1901 fewer than

200 million acres of the original 800 million acres of virgin forest in America remained undespoiled by wasteful and acquisative business interests; four-fifths of the timber in the United States had fallen into private hands, 10 percent of it owned by capitalist oligopolies in the form of the Southern Pacific Railroad, the Northern Pacific Railroad, and the Weyerhaeuser Timber Company.[6] Much the same conditions prevailed in the country's mineral and water resources.

This is not to say that earlier presidents had not made modest efforts to save our land from becoming corporately exploited. President Benjamin Harrison set aside the first forest reserves on behalf of the people in 1891. For his efforts senators under the influence of corporate lumber interests who favored the continued fouling of our natural resources to obtain commercial success threatened him with impeachment.[7]

It was in response to the Robber Baron morality of the fabulously rich corporations with their inexcusable waste and hard-hearted exploitation of natural resources and people alike that the Progressive movement began to take shape in the early 1890s. Progressivism challenged the myth of *laissez-faire* capitalism that had been the ideological cloak behind which big businessmen had hidden to establish their hammerlock on the nation's economic and political life during the last half of the nineteenth century.

It was natural, then, for the conservationists to fuse themselves with the Progressive movement in a effort to regulate the special interests that had poisoned both nature and the body politic from head to toe. The conservation movement, like the Progressive movement of which it was a part, was not a radical attack on capitalism bent on replacing it with a new socialist order.

Roosevelt himself, who more than any other man symbolized both movements, was a conservative patrician who understood and acted on what Alexis de Tocqueville called the principle of self-interest rightly understood. It is not a lofty principle and "everyone can without difficulty learn and retain it." It rests on the knowledge that one should at times sacrifice some of his private interests to save the rest.[8] It is a strategy of survival. As the aristocratic Tancredi advised his uncle, the Prince of Salina, when threatened with peasant revolution in Sicily, "If we want things to stay as they are, things will have to change."[9]

And so things did change in America as a result of the implementation of the principle of self-interest rightly understood by private corporations, politicians, and bureaucrats. Above all, the conservation movement was a scientific movement, frequently supported by the more enlightened corporations, which had as its philosophical linchpin "rational planning to promote efficient development and use of all natural resources." [10]

By yielding to the demands of Progressives and conservationists alike Roosevelt and the corporate interests managed to take away from the movement whatever revolutionary thunder it may have had. In the process they succeeded in withdrawing 150 million acres of forest land (an area larger than France) as a national forest reserve, in building dams to help irrigate and reclaim nearly 1.2 million more acres of arid land in the West (at the same time taming western opposition to his conservation program), and making Americans more conservation conscious by giving it wide publicity at the Washington Governor's Conference of 1908. Unlike the conservation movement of the 1960s and 1970s, the preservation of nature was seldom for its own sake, for this was a period of rapid economic growth. As such, the preservation of nature for its own sake was not deemed a practical policy. Its thrust was essentially developmental, more interested in the efficient conquest of nature rather than questioning the right of conquest itself. Conservation, said Gifford Pinchot, the father of American conservation, "stands against the waste of the natural resources which cannot be renewed . . . ; " [11] its first principle "is development, the use of natural resources now existing on this continent for the benefit of the people who live here now . . . , " [12] "and most of all it stands for an equal opportunity for every American citizen to get his fair share of benefit from these resources, both now and hereafter." [13]

The coming of World War I, coupled with a weariness of reform and the opposition of some of the less enlightened business interests to conservation, brought the first conservation movement to an end. As public attention shifted from domestic to foreign affairs, national priorities were reordered to favor national security and renewed capitalist despoliation of America's natural resources. "Normalcy" began to set in.

The second conservation movement came to life with the New Deal policies of President Franklin Roosevelt in 1933 in reaction to the Great Depression. Like its forerunner, its lifespan was terminated by war clouds as they began to form in the early 1940s.

It, too, was sparked by a historically imposed recognition of the limits of nature, though this time it was a Great Depression rather than the closing of the frontier that occasioned the awareness. Spurred by widespread economic dislocation, the devastation of the "Okies" and "Arkies" in the Dust Bowl of the Great Plains, and the rampaging flooding of the Tennessee River, Franklin Roosevelt followed his cousin's lead by instituting a program of public works designed to provide both employment and rational *regional* conservation of America's natural resources.

Like the first conservation movement, it was dominated by a "gospel of efficiency," which emphasized "development rather than preservation, and . . . man's control over his environment rather than [his] harmony with nature's forces." [14]

The spate of New Deal programs which came into existence ranged from the Tennessee Valley Authority and "shelter-belt" trees to protect the Dust Bowl area to the Civilian Conservation Corps designed to preserve and plant new forests. In these programs land was reclaimed, rivers were harnessed, and power generated. The emphasis was on the Keynesian philosophy of growth and expansion by scientifically managed capitalism and government planning.

Like his cousin, the second President Roosevelt was a Darwinian conservative bent on preserving the capitalist goose that laid the golden egg. The Communist Party, U.S.A., and the Socialist Party multiplied their memberships by hundreds and thousands of percent during the Republican administration of Herbert Hoover as he idly watched disillusionment with capitalism turn to despair. No doubt Arthur Schlesinger, Jr., is correct in concluding that Americans overestimated the peril of the "Red threat" and that if American Communists were following Marx during the thirties it was less Karl than Groucho. Nonetheless, the New Deal was an attempt to stem what was *perceived* to be a Red tide. The conservation part of that program was merely incidental to the larger concern of rescuing capitalism from the throes of depression.

The coming of World War II and the resistance of the business beneficiaries of the New Deal medicine forced Franklin Roosevelt to admit at a press conference on December 23, 1943, that the New

Deal had come to an end. So had what has been termed America's second conservation movement. Incrementally, it had added something new to the philosophy of the first conservation movement. Although accepting the principle of the *efficient* conquest of nature, it rejected the notion of the symbiotic equilibrium of nature in favor of *expansionism.*

Simply stated, the New Deal rejected the seesaw theory of capitalism which assumed that depressions would automatically bottom out and right themselves. Rather the New Deal programs assumed that the economy could go up or down and that the economy could rest like a becalmed ship at the bottom of the economic charts. Capitalism did not so much resemble a seesaw as an elevator, an elevator that "was just as capable of standing still on the ground floor as at the top of the shaft." [15]

Thus, the essence of the New Deal was to stimulate growth and expansion. People were urged to have larger families to produce an evergrowing market that would lead to an increased amount of employment and spending and which in turn would stimulate the growth of business. As late as the mid-1960s President Lyndon Baines Johnson was urging the American public to consume: it's good for the economy.

It is this pattern of our conservationist past that makes our conservationist present so interesting. Far from being quashed by a war (Vietnam, in this case), conservation or, to use the contemporary term, "ecology," stimulated by war, has forced us to look inward and to reflect on the sanity of our national priorities.

Its goals are also somewhat different. Rather than attempting to dominate nature to raise the level of American well-being by the expansion of our intake of natural resources, contemporary conservationists are urging antigrowth, zero-population, and diminished consumption.[16] This is not to say that our third conservation movement is unique. It is not. Rather it represents an evolutionary growth of the conservation movement based on the principle of self-interest rightly understood which has progressed from a *state* and *national* concern (evidenced by the Washington Governors Conference of 1908 and the Tennessee Valley Authority of 1933) to the *international* concern of the 1970s.

The conservationist movement of the 1970s also subscribes to the "gospel of efficiency" and recognizes the limits of nature, but, unlike its predecessors, it emphasizes that our planet is a closed system and that an environmental ripple in one part of the globe will have an impact on another.

Signifying the new international approach to America's third conservation movement was her participation in the 1972 United Nations Conference on the Human Environment held in Stockholm. Attended by 113 other nations, the conference resembled not so much a scientific convention as a summit conference. Plagued by politics of the Cold War and threatened by a boycott of the entire Soviet bloc, the Stockholm Conference nonetheless proved to be a remarkably productive meeting. Three major international environmental initiatives were agreed on.

First was an agreement to institute a 200-point program known as Earthwatch to monitor and improve the environment of the planet. Second, the Conference approved a plan to create a permanent U.N. secretariat to coordinate international environmental matters. Third, the Conference adopted an international declaration of accepted environmental principles.[17] Swedish sociologist and economist Gunnar Myrdal summed up the results when he commented: "I never expect anything from conferences, particularly international ones, but this one seems on the right track."[18]

That conclusion is not one shared by underdeveloped nations or by underdeveloped peoples in industrial countries in which the standard·of living is high. To countries that are banking on industrialization to raise their standard of living and international power the conservation movement sounds suspiciously like a plot on the part of the wealthy nations to prevent them from developing and competing for their fair share of nature's bounty.

The same holds true for underprivileged minority groups in the United States who tend to view the environmentalist issue as a rich white man's issue. For both the underdeveloped nations and the underprivileged peoples of the rich industrial nations conservation appears to be only the latest version of neo- or internal colonialism. To them the problem is not one of preventing man's tyranny of nature. Rather it is the historic problem of preventing nature and man alike from tyrannizing them. As one African delegate remarked after the Stockholm Conference:

> Our problem is not pollution due to industrial overdevelop-
> ment but poverty, plain and simple backwardness, and this
> conference will miss the boat unless it deals with the political
> regimes that keep things so.

It is not unrealistic to suggest that America's third conservation movement will also miss the boat unless it deals simultaneously with the problems of poverty and racism in America, for cleaner air, cleaner water, and conservation of our natural resources are not without costs, costs that are unevenly distributed throughout our population.

In 1972 the Nixon administration added 34 pieces of environmental legislation to the 3000 conservation bills already submitted to the Congress. Collectively these bills made up no less than 20 percent of the legislative agenda for that year. As a result the federal government spent more than $20 billion during the first two years of the 1970s to enforce laws that prohibited everything from open burning and ocean dumping to excessive noise from jet aircraft.

Thanks in part to the environmentalist lobby, the supersonic jetliner (SST) was scrapped, the Trans-Alaska Pipeline System (TAPS) blocked, and DDT outlawed for most uses. Such matters of public policy are not without their costs, particularly in terms of jobs. The White House Council on Environmental Quality (CEQ) expects that enforcement of conservation laws will result in as many as 300 plant closings in high polluting companies during the next five years. Because American ethnic minorities are the last to be hired and the first to be fired, this situation cannot help but exacerbate racial tensions in this country. See *Newsweek's* estimate of the cost of environmental cleanup in a few industries.

On the other hand, America cannot afford not to clean up her own as well as the global environment. It is important to remember the archaeological evidence that suggests that one factor in the decline of Rome was the systematic poisoning of upper class Romans by the lead with which they lined their wine containers.[19] Poisoning the atmosphere with lead is merely one of our present environmental problems.

Worse, we are well beyond the capabilities of what Kenneth Boulding called Spaceship Earth to support the life and demands

COUNTING THE COST

How much must U.S. industry spend to clean up air and water pollution? Estimates made for the White House Council on Environmental Quality suggest that the bill for 1972–76 will vary from one industry to the next. Among the hardest-hit producers, with the toll in jobs, idled plants and price increases:

Industry	Capital Investment	Annual Cost in 1975	Plants Closed	Jobs Lost	Added Cost to Customers
Electric utilities	$10.7 billion	$2.5 billion	None	None	7%
Pulp and paper	$3.3 billion	$5.50 to $12.50 per ton	90 to 100	16,000	3.5% to 10%
Petroleum refineries	$634 million to $1.1 billion	$21 million	12	1,000	8¢ per barrel
Aluminum smelters	$935 million	$290 million	None	None	5% to 8%
Iron foundries	$348 million	$125 million	400	8,000	1.7% to 5%
Copper smelters	$341 million	$95 million	2 by 1930	1,150	2½¢ per pound
Cement	$122 million	$43 million	25	?	4% to 5%
Leather tanneries	$89 million	$10.7 million	?	600	1% to 2%

Source: Newsweek (June 12, 1972), p. 48.

made on it by the inhabitants of the craft. Our spaceship is overloaded
by stresses placed on it by three different but related sources.

Our first overload is caused by population growth. As Robert
Heilbroner has noted, "the earth's passenger list is growing at a
rate that will give us some four billion humans by 1975 and . . .
threatens to give us eight billion by 2010," [20] which is only a generation away. Such steerage threatens to outstrip the ability of the earth
to yield a sufficient food supply to maintain life. A third of the
world already lives at the threshold of subsistence, and central American countries have fought wars literally for living space during the
last decade.[21] All of this portends not only the increased probability
of war between the rich and poor nations (or at a minimum between
the poor nations with all that it means in terms of the Cold War
struggle between the Soviet Union, the United States, and the Republic of China) but ecological disaster as well.

A second stress comes from the cumulative effect of the wastes
of our modern technology. Although the strain is now largely local-
ized, the effects on our shrinking world are spreading. Barry Commoner notes, for example, that nature cannot absorb our wastes as
fast as we are producing them. In the premodern world the environment provided an unlimited amount of clean air. Industrial wastes,
which produce carbon dioxide, have added nearly 14 percent of
the carbon-dioxide content of the air in the last 100 years to create
a modified "greenhouse" effect that traps the heat of the sun and
raises global temperatures. If global temperatures continue to rise,
it could bring about catastrophic consequences for the whole world.
One possibility would be a sequence of climatic changes that would
usher in a new Ice Age; another would be the melting of the Antarctic
ice cap which would produce a tidal wave that would wipe out
a large portion of humanity and swamp a great number of coastal
cities.[22]

A third threat to the limits of nature is the continued spread of
nuclear radiation which is stemming from the military experiments
of the French and Chinese as well as the possibility (one shudders
to think of probabilities) of a thermonuclear exchange between the
superpowers. Significantly, Professor Heilbroner notes that such an
exchange would have its most devastating effect in America's Northern
Hemisphere in which the resources of nature have been largely
expended.[23]

Thus the third American conservation movement is left between two tensions. On the one hand, it must pursue environmental reform or invite ecological disaster. On the other, such policies are likely to be counterproductive and face resistance from the underdeveloped parts of the world and underdeveloped parts of the rich nations unless their fate is considered. It may well be that the fate of the third American conservation movement, as well as the fate of mankind, hinges on the implementation of Tocqueville's principle of self-interest rightly understood.

Notes

1. See, for example, Van Rensselaer Potter, *Bioethics: Bridge To The Future* (Englewood Cliffs, New Jersey: Prentice-Hall, 1971), p 3

2. Barry Commoner, *Science & Survival* (New York: Viking, 1966), p. 3.

3. Reflecting the moorings of the present conservation movement to the white, middle-class intellectual, many college and university campuses celebrated "Earth Day" on April 22, 1970, to mold public opinion in support of ecology programs as well as question our national priorities in regard to Vietnam.

4. Timothy O'Riordan, "The Third American Conservation Movement," *Journal of American Studies* (August 1971), 155–171.

5. For an excellent history of the coalition which forged the first conservation movement see Samuel P. Hays, *Conservation And The Gospel Of Efficiency: The Progressive Conservation Movement, 1890–1920* (New York: Atheneum, 1969).

6. Samuel Eliot Morison and Henry Steele Commager, *The Growth of the American Republic*, II (New York: Oxford University Press, 1962), p 489

7. Robert Sherrill, *Why They Call It Politics* (New York: Harcourt Brace Jovanovich, 1972), p. 192.

8. Alexis de Tocqueville, *Democracy In America*, II (New York: Vintage, 1945), pp. 130–131.

9. Giuseppe di Lampedusa, *The Leopard* (New York: Pocket Books, 1967), p. 21.

10. Hays, *Conservation and the Gospel of Efficiency*, p. 2.

11. Benjamin Parke DeWitt, *The Progressive Movement* (Seattle: University of Washington Press, 1968), p. 51; found in Gifford Pinchot, *The Fight for Conservation*, p. 79.

12. Pinchot, *The Fight for Conservation*; quoted in O'Riordan, "The Third American Conservation Movement," p. 158.

13. DeWitt, *The Progressive Movement*, p. 51.

14. O'Riordan, "The Third Conservation Movement," p. 159.

15. Robert L. Heilbroner, *The Worldly Philosophers* (New York: Simon and Schuster, 1961), p. 235.

16. The entire issue of the August 1972 *Pacific Historical Review* is devoted to environmental history. Of particular interest is Lawrence Rakestraw's article "Conservation Historiography" and Michael McCloskey's "Wilderness Movement at the Crossroads, 1945–1970."

17. "109 Nations OK World Environment Statement," *Los Angeles Times,* Part I, June 17, 1972, p. 2.

18. "Environment '72: A Progress Report," *Newsweek News Pointer* (December 1972), 5.

19. Robert L. Heilbroner, "Ecological Armageddon," *New York Review of Books* (April 23, 1970), p. 3.

20. Heilbroner, "Ecological Armageddon," p. 3.

21. See Barbara Ward, *The Rich Nations And The Poor Nations* (New York: Norton, 1962).

22. Commoner, *Science & Survival,* pp. 10–11.

23. Heilbroner, "Ecological Armageddon," p. 3.

FROM EIGHT . . .

Just as man's abuse of technology has presented the greatest threat to our natural environment, likewise a similar misuse of technological innovations has led to flagrant violations of our civil liberties, as the Watergate scandal attests. In the first chapter, which dealt with the Puritan Ethic, it was shown how the level of technological development has shaped American values and behavior from the seventeenth century to the present. In this concluding chapter the role of technology is again high-lighted as readers take a futuristic look at "Civil Rights in the Twenty-First Century."

. . . ON TO NINE

A monarchy is like a merchantman. You get on board and ride the wind and tide, in safety and elation but by and by, you strike a reef and go down. But democracy is like a raft. You never sink, but, damn it, your feet are always in the water.[1]

Fisher Ames
The Federal Union

NINE

CIVIL RIGHTS IN THE TWENTY-FIRST CENTURY

FRED R. MABBUTT

So spoke Fisher Ames from the floor of the House of Representatives in 1795 as he watched with trepidation the new democratic government take form. He was, of course, wrong—democracies do sink—but he was most certainly correct in his understanding that "your feet are always in the water" in attempting to make democracy work.

Democracies are constantly being challenged externally by foreign powers and internally from within. They have no guardian angels, and for that reason must constantly ward against encroachments on the freedom that has been so hard won.

Democracy rests on the recognition of the dignity of the individual and on the assumption that men have, or may acquire, sufficient

intelligence and honesty to govern themselves. Freedom therefore
becomes an essential condition for the development of the individual
personality so that it may "translate itself from what it is to what
it has the capacity of becoming."[2] In this sense democratic government is a means toward an end and that end is freedom. As Herbert
Agar has put it, "It is freedom which men have always wanted and
upon which they must insist, for without freedom human beings
cannot become fully human."[3]

Yet there is a tendency for all governments, democratic or not,
to refrain from vigorously promoting the freedom of its citizenry
because freedom is a nuisance to the administration of government.
Paradoxically, individual freedom may be even more stiffled in a
democratic state than in one that is authoritarian. Remarking on
this point while observing *Democracy in America* during the 1830's,
Alexis de Tocqueville wrote:

> The authority of a king is purely physical, and it controls the
> actions of the subject without subduing his private will; but
> the majority [in a democracy] possesses a power which is
> physical *and* moral at the same time; it acts upon the will
> as well as upon the actions of men and it represses not only
> all contests, but all controversy.[4]

In other words, public opinion in a democracy is so powerful that
it literally obliterates the *will* of the individual to exercise his freedom
to differ from the popular opinions of the day. Because of this,
Tocqueville feared that the ruling majority would attempt to impose
conformity on the individual citizen and that democratic nations
would become "nothing better than a flock of timid and industrious
animals, of which the government is the shepherd."[5] The fears of
Tocqueville have not proved unfounded as Americans approach the
twenty-first century.

Freedom and Conformity
in the Twenty-First Century

Men who collect together to form a majority do not suddenly become
virtuous or change their characters. Moreover, there is no guarantee

that people living under a democratic form of government will not succumb to folly or hysteria and vote themselves into slavery like the people of Germany in 1933 when they elevated Adolph Hitler to the position of chancellor.

Recognizing this possibility, the Founders of this nation added a Bill of Rights to the Constitution—the purpose of which was to protect the freedom of the individual who differs from the popular opinions of the day. They foresaw correctly that the ruling majority might attempt to cloak its self-interest in the flag and curtail any criticism of its policies by labeling them unpatriotic or even treasonable. "My country right or wrong" is not a form of speech that will have need of the First Amendment's protection of the freedom of speech.

However, individual freedom, though enshrined in such documents as the Bill of Rights, is never secure. Indeed, a Bill of Rights is only parchment and may be repealed or restricted in a democratic system if that is the will of the people. That this is a real possibility in the United States today was recently revealed in a nation-wide poll conducted by CBS News, which concluded that a majority of Americans favor conformity over freedom and indicate a willingness to restrict some of the basic freedoms constitutionally guaranteed by the Bill of Rights.[6]

Progress is not a law of nature and nothing stands still in politics. Slowly, and with many lapses, we have developed the freedom embodied in the Bill of Rights; but we can slump back in a few complaisant years to the status of subjects rather than free men.

Adverse public opinion, however, is not the only challenge posed to freedom in the United States. Throughout man's history technological and scientific developments have challenged the delicate balance between freedom and conformity in political systems. These developments may prove to be a boon or a bane to society, depending on *how* they are applied by man. Yet one thing is certain: science causes change and political systems will feel the stress of adjustment. This is not a new phenomenon. Indeed, one need only recall Socrates, western civilization's "first scientist," who challenged the political system in Athens by undermining the myth on which that city-state rested, namely that Zeus was god and the founder of the city. In *The Clouds* Aristophanes, his contemporary, provides posterity with an account of the scientific challenge to the politics of that day.

SOCRATES.	Zeus! What Zeus? Are you mad? There is no Zeus.
STREPSIADES.	What are you saying now? Who causes the rain to fall? Answer me that!
SOCRATES.	Why, 'tis these, and I will prove it. Have you ever seen it raining without clouds? Let Zeus then cause rain with a clear sky and without their presence!
STREPSIADES.	By Apollo! that is powerfully argued! For my own part, I always thought it was Zeus pissing into a sieve. But tell me, who is it makes the thunder, which I so much dread?
SOCRATES.	'Tis these, when they roll one over the other.
STREPSIADES.	But how can that be? You most daring among men!
SOCRATES.	Being full of water, and forced to move along, they are of necessity precipitated in rain, being fully distended with moisture from the regions where they have been floating; hence they bump each other heavily and burst with great noise.
STREPSIADES.	But is it not Zeus who forces them to move?
SOCRATES.	Not at all; 'tis the aerial Vortex.[7]

During the Middle Ages no doubt the invention of the stirrup, which allowed an armored knight to stay on his mount, powerfully lent itself to the principle of political inequality and authoritarianism in much the same fashion that gunpowder and the bullet lent themselves later to the principle of equality and freedom. The point is simply that scientific-technological change produces political change for better or for worse and that never before in man's history has there been an era in which science has enjoyed so much success. Indeed, one Harvard professor has computed that among the scientists deemed significant by the world, 90 percent are alive today.[8] It is clear that Americans are living in an age of science, and this cannot fail to have an affect on American politics and, in particular, on the individual freedoms found in the Bill of Rights.

The question then becomes: how will science and technology alter the political landscape in the United States? Will this new technology prove to be our slave or our master? The truth is that in our time freedom is being both strengthened and weakened by the new science and technology. This apparent contradiction may be seen if we survey the dimensions of our various freedoms. Because space does not permit an exhaustive examination of all our freedoms, a selective examination of a few will serve to suggest the nature of this apparent contradiction as we approach the twenty-first century.

First, it must be noted that our rights may have a *positive* as well as a *negative* side. In the area of the right to speak, for example, we are not only guaranteed the positive exercise of that freedom but also its negative counterpart—the right to silence.[9] The impact of science and technology is dramatic and has broadened our ability to enjoy this right in such devices as the telephone, telegraph, and television. With the penetration of man into outer space and the introduction of Telstar devices to broaden our ability to communicate instantly with our neighbors abroad, the expansion of this freedom has been phenomenal.

Yet there is a more sinister side to the use of technology in the area of free speech, for that same technology may be used to stifle it and to exact conformity to the opinions of the majority which control our government. Consider, for example, the testimony of Dr. Jerome B. Weisner of M.I.T., as he testified before the 1971 Senate Judiciary Committee investigating the problem of governmental eavesdropping and surveillance of individuals active in American politics.

Modern information technology provides the potential to add to our general well-being and to enhance human freedom and dignity, if properly used, by extending our muscles, brainpower and material resources, and yet it also threatens to ensnarl us in a social system in which controls could essentially eliminate human freedom and individual dignity.

Improperly exploited computer and communication technology could so markedly restrict the range of individual rights and initiatives that are the hallmark of a free society and the foundations of human dignity as to eliminate meaningful life as we appreciate it. In other words, *1984* could come to pass unnoticed while we applauded our technical achievements . . .

I suspect that it would be much easier to guard against a malicious oppressor than to avoid being slowly but increasingly dominated by an information Frankenstein of our own creation.[10]

The subject of the Senate inquiry was the ominous invasion of liberty carried on, in the name of constitutionalism and law and order, to equate dissent with lawlessness and nonconformity with treason. Just how far this has gone is hard to say, but one gets an idea when it is discovered that military and civilian authorities have used electronic devices to monitor the activities of such critics as Senator Adlai Stevenson III, Representative Abner Mikva, federal appellate judge Otto Kerner, the Reverend Ralph Abernathy, and Louisiana congressman Hale Boggs. This type of military and governmental electronic eavesdropping has, as one judge put it, "a chilling effect" on peaceful political activities and makes it no longer possible to dismiss such works as *1984* and *Brave New Worlds* as mere literary nightmares.[11]

Already the government holds large dossiers on a major part of the population. Most Americans are unaware of the extent to which governmental agencies are using computers and microfilm to collect information about the activities of private citizens. New York State is developing a statewide police information network which all authorities agree could be extended across the nation within a brief time.[12] With computers and such scientific innovations as "radio pills" which, when swallowed, turn a person into a human broadcasting system, it is quite possible to assert an almost continuous surveillance over every citizen.

A second freedom that has felt the impact of technology is the right to one's property which is guaranteed in both the Fifth and Fourteenth Amendments. Again this right has been expanded because of the productive power of technology. America's economic power has produced what John Kenneth Galbraith has called "the affluent society," a society made so rich by technology that one economist has projected that the average income of all families and unattached individuals will be $15,000 a year by the year 2000.[13] Already it is nearing the $10,000 mark.

The United States has emerged as the most prosperous nation on earth, giving vastly more Americans an opportunity to enjoy their Fifth and Fourteenth Amendment protection of property. Since the setback of the Great Depression of the 1930s Americans have witnessed a steady increase in their production, income, and consumption. Whether one measures the output of industrial and agricultural production, the increase in productivity per man-hour or the wages received for work, the United States either leads its nearest foreign rival or is not far behind. Indeed, Dr. Linus Pauling, a Nobel Prize winning scientist, estimates that 3 billion poor people living outside the United States have a national income of $200,000,000,000, which is equivalent to the income received by the richest one-twentieth of the American population, and that Americans, who constitute only 6 percent of the world's population, possess almost two-thirds of the world's wealth.[14] Never before have so many Americans had so much abundance and never before has the property right been so expanded.

Yet, as the 1964 Report of the Senate Subcommittee on Employment and Manpower noted, a "manpower revolution" has been created. Somewhere in the 1950s the American economy broke through a technological barrier and introduced automation (i.e., self-correcting machines that feed back information and adjust themselves) and cybernation (i.e., hooking those machines to one another so that they are self-operating), all of which made it possible to expand production of goods while reducing the labor force.

A few examples may serve to demonstrate this point. In 1964 it took only 10 men to produce the same number of automobile motor blocks that required 400 men 10 years earlier. Two men could make a thousand radios a day, whereas it took 200 only a few years before. Fourteen men could operate the glass-blowing machines that manufactured 90 percent of all the glass bulbs in the United States.[15] As a result of technological gains, America's agricultural abundance permitted Americans to spend less of their income on food than any other nation in the world, while reducing the rural farming population from 14 to 7 percent, and led to a public program of price supports designed to curb production.

This trend illuminates an economic and, by implication, political paradox: the coexistence of prosperity and chronic unemployment. The new technology has drastically reduced the unskilled and semi-skilled industrial jobs, but it has also affected white-collar areas. Herbert Simon has observed that by 1985 automation can do away with all middle management.[16] Since middle management is considered the ultimate goal of much of America's middle class, this indeed would have profound results. Other observers, like Ben Seligman, are even gloomier—estimating a job loss of 40,000 a week, or 2 million a year, because of automation.[17] At this rate the work force would be completely abolished by the year 2000. Reacting to these predictions, the national government has emphasized in recent years programs like "manpower retraining" to avoid what former Secretary of Labor Willard Wirtz has termed "dead-end jobs."

Although statistics do not show that work as we know it is actually being abolished—employment has, for example, increased in the tertiary sector in such areas as teaching and hospital work—they certainly suggest that it is in the realm of possibility in the not-too-distant future. Economists of both liberal and conservative persuasion have advocated a "guaranteed minimum income" or a "negative income tax" to establish a minimum income floor for those who lose their jobs to technology. President Nixon's poverty program reflects this concern. In particular, his family assistance plan represents a modified version of the guaranteed income idea. As the President explained it, his plan would provide a federal foundation "under the income of every American family with dependent children that cannot care for itself." Although the bill has not passed the Senate Finance Committee, it is clear from the wide margin of approval given by the House that in time it will pass and thus create a new kind of property association or relationship.

In the seventeenth century James Harrington wrote a classic book entitled *The Commonwealth of Oceana*, which dealt with the relations between property and power. In that volume Harrington raised one of the oldest problems of government: how can people without property be genuinely free? Echoing this concern, James Madison wrote in *The Federalist*, "Power over a man's support is power over his will." John Adams compressed this thought into three words: "Power follows property."

In other words, if an increasing number of people are to be on the roll of a government dole, can they use their freedom of speech or assembly if they are in danger of losing their paychecks when the government disagrees? If society becomes split into the highly educated who run the technocracy and the government on the one side and the passive, consuming mass on the other, can a democracy be maintained? What will replace work for the unemployed? Bread and circuses? Will America face a dictatorship of the technocrats?

These are weighty questions that cannot be answered easily. At best it alerts our generation that the discoveries of science are amoral and that they in no way guarantee human progress. How they are used—whether for welfare or warfare—depends solely on human choice and direction.

A third freedom affected by the impact of science and technology is the guarantee to "life" that may not be denied without "due process of law," i.e., without fair law and fair judicial procedures. Science has again dramatically broadened this right to life by not only lengthening the lifespan of most Americans but by improving the quality of life in the elimination of disease and deformities.

Already some Americans are beginning to talk about their "unalienable right" to life-saving devices such as the kidney machine, and the question whether a "donor" must consent to give his body organisms after death or whether the state may take them without consent has already been raised.[18] Indeed, scientists are challenging the legal definition of life and death itself when they ask when a patient is legally dead so that his heart or kidney may be extracted in its best condition for transplantation. Artificial insemination has raised the opposite question: what is legitimate life?[19] Because many states do not permit illegitimate children to inherit property, the status of some 10,000 children a year who are conceived by such means is in doubt until the courts come to an agreement on a definition of "legitimate" life.

Moreover, science is now beginning to unlock the fundamental life processes. As Dr. Robert Sisheimer of Caltech has noted: "For the first time in all time, a living creature understands its origin and can undertake to design its future."[20] In the near future, with genetic medicine, science may be able to eliminate harmful genes that may be the cause of such congenital illnesses and deformities as cystic fibrosis, diabetes, mongolism, and hydrocephalus. As life lengthens, we may expect new social needs and "rights" in such areas as medical attention, income maintenance, and recreation.

Yet, although there is nothing romantic about a mongoloid child or a disease-ridden body, this progress clearly opens the door to the possibility of human engineering. Physicians already see the possibility of artificial involution, i.e., the fertilization of eggs in a test tube which would then be replanted in the human female uterus. Test-tube babies, once the realm of science fiction, are now not only possible but even probable.

Indeed, scientists at the National Heart Institute have already experimented with an "artificial womb" and have managed to keep lamb fetuses alive in it for more than two days. Once this apparatus is perfected, the baby hatcheries of *Brave New World* would cease to be myth and become reality.

Further, medical researchers have succeeded in reproducing DNA, the chemical substance that carries the human genetic message which determines the sex and makeup of the newborn. Dr. J. B. Gurdon of Oxford University has used unfertilized eggs to "clone" or repro-duce the genetic twin of a tadpole from the original egg. Scientists are now arguing that one day man may reproduce himself asexually in the same way by creating identical twins "from a test tube full of cells carried through gestation by donor mothers or hatched in an artificial womb." [21] In such an actuality individual behavior may become far less free and spontaneous and more subject to deliberate "programming." As we become increasingly capable of determining the sex, intelligence, and genetic makeup of our children, there may be a tendency to sacrifice individuality on the altar of conformity. Some have argued that television will add to this condition by reducing sectional differences in dress, customs, speech, and values, which, in turn, would add fuel to the fires of conformity and produce future problems in the area of censorship and freedom of speech.

Given the impact of these and other scientific developments, we are led to wonder what traditional rights will be challenged and what new rights or freedoms may emerge as Americans approach the twenty-first century.

The Forgotten Ninth Amendment: A New Magna Charta of Freedom?

Some have argued that part of the Constitution contains a forgotten but significant new Magna Charta of American freedom which may give to that document the needed elasticity to adjust to the challenges of science and technology. In Bennett R. Patterson's book on *The Forgotten Ninth Amendment* it is suggested that this amendment represents "a solemn declaration that natural rights are not a fixed category" but rather "a declaration of the sovereignty and dignity of the individual" and the inherent freedom necessary to maintain that dignity.[22]

Echoing the concern of the *Declaration of Independence* for the "unalienable rights" of man, the Ninth Amendment reads:

> The enumeration in the Constitution, of certain rights, shall not be construed to deny or disparage others retained by the people.

It is clear from this statement, and the earlier draft of the Ninth Amendment, that James Madison, its author, was not *merely* placing another limitation on the powers of the federal government but that this amendment was a declaration of understanding that inherent human rights are not enumerated.

Because the rights guaranteed under the Ninth Amendment are not spelled out, the only way to discover what they are is by a process of elimination of known rights. Not included would be the enumerated powers in the Constitution, those sections like the Bill of Rights and the Fourteenth Amendment that limit the power of the state and federal government or those that specify the powers remaining to the people. The rights found within the Ninth Amendment would, in turn, be conditioned, if not determined, by the developments of science and technology. What, then, is the forecast for the development of new rights for Americans in the twenty-first century and what may be the future application of the Ninth Amendment?

Forecasting is a dangerous business and the forecaster has never been a popular figure. Indeed, it may be recalled that Dante Alighieri reserved the Eighth Circle of his *Inferno* for forecasters for venturing into the future, which belonged to God alone. With their heads twisted completely around, they were unable to see where they were going. No doubt, as Herman Miller has suggested, this is "the reason forecasters to this day continue to have their heads screwed on backward. It is only by looking at the past that they can tell the future."[23]

What, then, is the past and what may be the future?

As we have seen, rights are in flux because of the almost exponential impact of science on law. Until recently there has been little reason to tap the unenumerated rights guaranteed to Americans under the Ninth Amendment. Indeed, the Ninth Amendment was not even cited by the Supreme Court for 175 years, essentially because the Court was relatively unchallenged by the explosion of knowledge so characteristic of our age, thus allowing it to believe that all basic rights were covered in the first eight amendments.

The only important case yet decided by use of the Ninth Amendment occurred in 1965 in *Griswold v. Connecticut*.[24] In a 7 to 2 decision, the Supreme Court overruled an 1879 law that forbade the use of contraceptive devices to prevent birth.

In the *Griswold* case the defendants, cosponsors of a birth control clinic, cited the First, Fourth, Fifth, Ninth, and Fourteenth Amendments in their charge that the law was an invasion of privacy.

In Justice William O. Douglas' majority opinion the Ninth Amendment was cited.

> We deal with a right of privacy older than the Bill of Rights— older than our political parties, older than our school system. Marriage is a coming together for better or for worse, hopefully enduring, and intimate to the degree of being sacred. The association promotes a way of life, not causes; a harmony in living, not political faiths; a bilateral loyalty, no commercial or social projects. Yet it is an association for as noble a purpose as any involved in our prior decision.[25]

In a concurring opinion Justices Arthur Goldberg and William Brennan and Chief Justice Warren asserted that the Ninth Amendment protects certain fundamental rights not listed in the Bill of Rights which includes the right to privacy in marriage. Justice Goldberg used Mr. Patterson's *The Forgotten Ninth Amendment* to substantiate this claim of marital privacy.[26]

Application of the Ninth Amendment in the future seems to be assured, and there has been much speculation concerning possible areas of use. Mr. Patterson feels that the Ninth Amendment includes the *Declaration of Independence*'s guarantee to the rights of life, liberty, and the pursuit of happiness, plus the rights of security, property, freedom of conscience, freedom of contract, and freedom to engage in a profession, trade, or business.[27] He believes that the

Ninth Amendment will guard private or personal rights rather than public or group rights and that it should be used as a counterpart to the General Welfare clause of the Preamble to the Constitution, which states the purpose of the Constitution to be group welfare. If the Ninth Amendment were viewed as protecting public rights, the rights of the individual would be even more obscured than in the past and would be lost in conformity from an essentially egalitarian society.

As Mr. Patterson observed:

> The psychological fact is that to the mass of men, acting as a whole, liberty is primarily the removal of restraint on crowd behavior, and what the crowd calls liberty is not liberty for the individual; it is liberty for the crowd to act without considering the results of their behavior on other people.[28]

Although it is clear that the Founding Fathers intended the Ninth Amendment to protect the individual from the oppression of an autocratic majority, it may prove equally important in the future in the protection of the individual from the pressures of conformity that may attend our age of science.

The problem of balancing freedom with conformity in the age of science may possibly be eased by the presence and future application of the Ninth Amendment. Cases like that of *Loving v. Virginia* (1967), which knocked down state laws forbidding interracial marriages, might well have used the Ninth Amendment rather than the Fourteenth to guarantee "unlisted rights," including the right to choose one's marriage partner.[29]

New rights are on the horizon. Already cases claiming the "right" to a cloud—inconceivable before science made the seeding of rainclouds possible—and the "right" to leave property to children conceived by artificial insemination are or have been before the courts of law. Here, too, the Ninth Amendment may ease the adjustment of America to the realities of scientific advances as it enters the twenty-first century.[30] In this modern age of science the Ninth Amendment may well prove to be a great centurion of our traditional as well as our new individual freedoms. As one writer put it, "Those who regard the invasion of the individual's privacy . . . as one of the great threats of our time may come to regard" the Ninth Amendment as "the Magna Charta" of our time.[31]

Notes

1. John D. Hicks, *The Federal Union* I (New York: Houghton Mifflin, 1937), p. 217.
2. Herbert Agar, *The Perils of Democracy* (New York: Capricorn, 1968), p. 18.
3. *Ibid.*
4. Alexis de Tocqueville, *Democracy in America*, I (New York: Vintage, 1945), p. 273.
5. *Ibid.*
6. James Reston, "Washington: Repeal the Bill of Rights?" *The New York Times*, April 18, 1970.
7. Aristophanes, *Complete Plays of Aristophanes* (New York: Simon and Schuster, 1967), p. 282.
8. Robert Heilbroner, *The Worldly Philosophers* (New York: Simon and Schuster, 1967), p. 282.
9. *Watkins v. United States*, 354 U.S. 178 (1957).
10. *Los Angeles Times*, March 21, 1971.
11. Mark Arnold, "Fears of Government Snooping to Get New Airing," *The National Observer*, February 22, 1971.
12. Francois Duchens, Ed., *The Endless Crisis* (New York: Simon and Schuster, 1970), pp. 192–198.
13. Herman P. Miller, *Rich Man, Poor Man* (New York: Crowell, 1971), pp. 240–243.
14. Linus Pauling, "Table Talk," *The Center Magazine* (Santa Barbara, California: Center for the Study of Democratic Institutions), I (September 1968), 246.
15. Michael Harrington, *The Accidental Century* (Baltimore, Maryland: Penguin, 1969), pp. 246–247.
16. Charles R. Dechert, Ed., *The Social Impact of Cybernetics* (New York: Simon and Schuster, 1966), pp. 36–69.
17. *Ibid.*
18. South Africa, for example, has already passed such a law whereby body organisms may be extracted after death with or without the donor's consent. In a country committed to an Apartheid policy only time will tell the consequences.
19. "The Riddle of Artificial Insemination," *Time* (February 25, 1966), 48.
20. "Man Into Superman," *Time* (April 19, 1971), 33.
21. *Ibid.*, 38.
22. Roscoe Pound, in Bennett Patterson, *The Forgotten Ninth Amendment* (Indianapolis: Bobbs-Merrill, 1955), p. iv.

23. *Miller, Rich Man, Poor Man,* p. 234.
24. *Griswold v. Connecticut,* 381 U.S. 479 (1965); for an earlier analysis of the Ninth Amendment see Knowlton H. Kelsey, "The Ninth Amendment of the Federal Constitution," *Indiana Law Journal,* **XI** (April 1936), 319.
25. *Griswold v. Connecticut,* p. 486.
26. *Ibid.,* p. 490.
27. Patterson, *Forgotten Ninth Amendment,* p. 23.
28. *Ibid.,* p. 57.
29. *Ibid.*
30. Gordon MacDonald, "Science and Politics of Rainmaking," *Bulletin of the Atomic Scientists,* **XXIV,** No. *8* (October 1968), 8–14.
31. James D. Carrol, "The Forgotten Amendment," *Nation,* CCI (September 6, 1965), 122.

INDEX

161

About the Authors

THOMAS J. OSBORNE is chairman of the department of history at Santa Ana College. He served as assistant professor of history, Chapman College World Campus Afloat, in 1970. His articles have appeared in the *Oregon Historical Quarterly, Southern California Quarterly, Thought, Colorado Quarterly,* and the *Texas Quarterly.*

FRED R. MABBUTT is chairperson of the department of political science at Santa Ana College. He received his Ph. D. in political science from Claremont Graduate School and University Center. He is coauthor of *Paths to the Present* and has published numerous articles.

DATE DUE

DEMCO 38-296